EXAMINING OUR TIMES

For the Way We Live Now

Over 100,000 copies of Tony Humphreys' books have already sold in the English language.

Books by Tony Humphreys

The Family: Love It and Leave It

A Different Kind of Teacher

A Different Kind of Discipline

The Power of 'Negative' Thinking

Myself, My Partner

Work and Worth: Take Back Your LIfe

Self-esteem: The Key to Your Child's Future

Children Feeling Good

Audio-tapes and CDs by Tony Humphreys

Self-esteem for Adults

Raising Your Child's Self-esteem

Embrace Failure

EXAMINING OUR TIMES
For the Way We Live Now

Tony Humphreys

Newleaf

Newleaf
an imprint of
Gill & Macmillan Ltd
Hume Avenue, Park West
Dublin 12
with associated companies throughout the world
www.gillmacmillan.ie

© Tony Humphreys 2002
0 7171 3452 0

Design and print origination by
Carrigboy Typesetting Services, Co. Cork
Printed by ColourBooks Ltd, Dublin

This book is typeset in 11.5/15pt Rotis.

The paper used in this book comes from the wood pulp of managed forests.
For every tree felled, at least one tree is planted, thereby renewing natural
resources.

A CIP catalogue record for this book is available from the British Library.

5 4 3 2 1

CONTENTS

PART THREE EDUCATION

PART FOUR SELF

PART FIVE WORK

PART SIX WELL-BEING

INTRODUCTION

The pieces in this book were originally written for the *Irish Times* and the *Irish Examiner.* My columns in both newspapers have been a way of reaching a readership interested in the impact of cultural changes on our everyday lives. They have allowed me to explore the ways we can cope with change both inside ourselves and between others and ourselves. A dialogue between readers and myself often emerged following a particular piece, and the exchange of ideas and differences were of considerable value to the further development of many of my ideas.

The rapid development of a pluralist and multi-racial culture in Ireland has led to a necessary re-evaluation of how we relate, educate, work, pray and recreate. Changing times means challenging times. On the one hand, pluralism provides opportunities for liberation, but on the other hand it brings confusion, doubt and insecurity. There are parents who worry about what are the best child-rearing practices and what are the values we need to pass on to our children. Children have a lot more power and visibility but these healthy developments have led to a breaking down of what in many cases were questionable discipline procedures in homes and schools. Parents and teachers are struggling to find more mature ways of bringing about responsible behaviours in their children.

Whilst in many ways children themselves are gaining from the changes in our culture, in other ways they are losing out. Due to the high rate of marital breakdown, children are experiencing a considerably shorter period of stable family life, and even when their parents do part they continue to be distressed because of the continuation of conflict between their parents.

Lone-parenting families now account for 30 to 40 per cent of families, and the influence of this on both the parents and children has yet to be assessed. The influence of child-minders (who often see a lot more of children than their parents do) also requires evaluation.

In terms of relationships, fewer women want to marry, as equality has not yet been achieved in marital and family life. Women still take 90 per cent of the responsibility for home-making and for child rearing. Married career women have far less leisure time than married men, are more prone to depression and anxiety and have reduced life expectancy.

Work has become a dominant aspect of many adults' lives. For many the working week has crept up to a forty-five hour week. In the workplace, expectations of employees have heightened but, equally, employees have become more assertive about their rights to physical, emotional, social and sexual safety.

There is quite a push on men to find their feminine side and women to realise their masculine side. Both men and women are expected to be independent, to understand concepts of self-worth and self-esteem, to be able to develop more mature relationships with others, to be emotionally literate, environ-mentally aware and physically fit and healthy. Quite a tall order for members of a culture that heretofore punished indi-viduality, rewarded conformity, insisted that couples 'lie in the bed they made' and reared boys to be boys and girls to be girls.

Religious practice is in deep decline and the search for spiritual meaning has gone beyond the limited confines of the traditional religions.

There has been a startling rise in the demand for psychotherapy, counselling and family therapy. Not only has the medical model of psychiatry come under major scrutiny, the shortcomings of general medicine are also being highlighted. Indeed, all the health and welfare services are experiencing major challenges to respond to the needs of a more vocal and educated populace.

I am grateful to my readers for supporting my columns and for their engagement with them. I am optimistic for the future and I hope that these pieces will be helpful in taking on the challenges facing us so that we can all participate in the development of a vibrant, productive, creative, caring and spiritual New Ireland.

PART ONE
RELATIONSHIPS

- Making sense of attraction
- Listening is an act of worship
- Addiction to caring
- The power of anger
- Beyond forgiveness
- Living from your head
- Men in crisis
- Do mothers-in-law ruin marriages?
- Separated but not gone
- The violence of silence
- The end of marriage!
- What men really want
- Saving marriage

MAKING SENSE OF ATTRACTION

Do you as husband or wife or parent hear yourself talking and think, 'I sound just like my mother (or father)', or do you find yourself doing things in the same way as your mother or father? Do you find that your marriage relationship repeats that of your parents in certain ways?

Maybe sometimes, during arguments with your partner, you shout: 'You're just like your mother (or father).' Perhaps as a parent you find yourself repeating the sad patterns of irritability, ridiculing, scolding, comparing, threatening and so on that you experienced at the hands of your parents as a child? Or maybe you find yourself doing exactly the opposite of what your parents did with you – which can be just as problematic.

Unless you develop awareness, the probability is high that as a partner in a couple relationship and as a parent you will either repeat or directly oppose the patterns of relating that existed in your family of origin. This is not surprising, for many reasons: for example, these are the patterns that are most familiar to you.

However, the major purpose of repeat patterns is to get you as an adult to face unresolved issues from your childhood and to face the continuation of childish dependence in your adulthood. You are likely to marry a partner who resembles the parent by whom you felt most hurt. In doing that, you are faced once again with the neglect that was present in how your parents related to you. But now as an adult, unlike the child who is always at the mercy of home and other circumstances, you have a second chance to redeem yourself from the unloving aspects of your parents' relationship with you. An example will clarify these processes.

A frequently occurring relationship is where a man who is aggressive, dominant, critical and controlling marries a woman who is passive, people-pleasing, non-assertive and docile. In such a relationship, the man may be like his father and have married a woman like his mother. The woman may be like her own mother and have married a man like her own father. Both parties in this newly formed relationship have come from problematic families of origin. The likelihood that they will create a happy family is low. Why, in this case, would the man choose to marry a woman like his mother, who, after all, did not protect him against the wrath and abuse of his aggressive father?

The purpose is threefold:

- to face his father within himself
- to face his mother within his wife
- to change the patterns of relating to self, partner, others and children.

This man's wife, who is likely to have married someone like her father and who is herself like her own mother, is also faced with similar responsibilities:

- to face her mother within herself
- to face her father within her husband
- to change the patterns of relating to self, partner, others and children.

The man's first task is to face the father within himself. He has to stand back from his aggressive behaviours and ask: 'Why am I using these same means of relating to others as my father did in his relationships with me?' He needs to return to his childhood and witness again the effects of his father's behaviour on himself, on his mother and on other family members. He needs to feel the fear, hurt, humiliation, anger and helplessness that he experienced as a child so that he can be determined that he will not expose his children, himself and his partner to such sad experiences. Most of all, he needs to learn to love and care for himself in a way that both his parents were unable to do.

Likewise, the wife who is passive, timid and fearful needs to ask herself: 'Why am I as a grown-up adult using these same ways of relating to others as my mother did in her relationship with my father, with myself and others?' She too needs to return to her childhood and experience again the effects of her father's dominance and her mother's passive behaviours on her. She needs to see how she as a small child would have felt frightened, abandoned by both parents and helpless, and how she protected herself by being 'good and passive' (like her mother). Out of this understanding she can determine to let go of these passive ways so that she as a mother does not abandon her children to a fate of being bullied and dominated or neglected because of passivity on her part. Like her spouse, she needs to become the positive parent towards herself that she missed in her own childhood.

Unless partners become aware of the enduring influence that troubled families can have on them, the danger is that dependent and neglectful relationship patterns will be repeated in the couple and later on in the family relationships.

Awareness is a necessary prerequisite to change, but unless it is coupled with determined, persistent alternative action that enhances personal, couple and family well-being, then it will not bring about the desired change.

LISTENING IS AN ACT OF WORSHIP

The first act of communication is listening. Many individuals that I have helped to overcome social phobias express fears of not being able to start and maintain a conversation. What often helps is when I explain that what most people need in company is someone to listen, to understand, to empathise and to show interest in their presence and their lives.

While there are many people who are good at talking, and some who dominate conversations so that nobody can get a word in edgeways, people who are good at listening are thin on the ground, even though the basis of forming meaningful contact with others is active listening. Active listening is when you listen with both mind and heart and demonstrate spontaneous physical, social and emotional responses to what the other person is saying. Active listening not only takes note of what is being verbally said but also notes the array of non-verbal messages that accompany verbalisations. Examples are tone of voice, facial expression, mannerisms, body posture, eye movements, affective state (flat, hostile, distressed, tense, depressed). Furthermore, the person who actively listens also listens to self by observing his own internal and external reactions to what the other person is saying. However, whilst self-listening is necessary so that the person stays in tune with what is happening within himself, the person who is good at listening does not allow this information to distract him from his focus on the other. He may mentally note that there is something he will need to consider later on or he may wait for an opportunity to voice his reactions, but not at the expense of the other.

There are many behaviours that block effective listening:

- non-listening
- 'wanting my turn'
- moralising
- advice-giving
- the 'me-too syndrome'
- anxiety
- fatigue
- present psychosocial state

The most hurtful of the above responses is non-listening. I recall a man telling me that it suddenly dawned on him when he was four years of age that his mother never listened to him. Four-year-olds need to ask a lot of questions in order to understand the complex world they live in; my client stopped asking. In his mid-thirties he had many questions that required answering. He also needed to be helped to listen to himself.

The 'wanting my turn' is a very common listening stopper. This is when a person cannot wait to express his own views and rarely allows the other person the time or opportunity to expand their ideas. Such behaviour springs from a person's own insecurities and drive to be seen and heard by others. These individuals are not in a place of readiness to listen and are rarely a good source of support.

Moralising is an attempt by the person who is listening to impose his or her own value system onto the speaker and, not surprisingly, it is guaranteed to dry up the spontaneity and disclosures being made by the speaker. I remember a woman telling me that she had gone to her family doctor to get help for her failing marriage and her confusion around feeling attracted to another man. She found herself being quickly put in her place by the doctor's response: 'Your place is with your husband and children.' Needless to say, she did not return to the doctor.

There is a wise rule of thumb when listening to another and that is to never give advice unless it is requested, and even when requested, offer suggestions but not advice. Advice-giving is putting yourself in the superior position of 'I know what is best for you', and it carries an implicit criticism of the ability of the speaker to find their own solutions and conclusions. Those who give advice often have an addiction to being needed.

The 'me-too syndrome' is a major communication stopper, because the person who is listening really only wants to talk about himself, and no matter what the other person says, he will find a way to relate it to himself – 'Let me tell you about my experience' or 'You think you've had it bad . . . ' are typical examples. People who slip into 'me-too responses' generally have an overwhelming drive to be listened to, and until this is resolved they are unlikely to become effective at active listening.

Anxiety makes it very difficult to listen to another. For example, if you are unsure of yourself, or if you are anxious about an examination, you are not in a place to listen. What would help here is the voicing of your anxiety and, hope-fully, the other person will be in a place to listen and support you.

Energy is vital to listening, and fatigue as a listening stopper speaks for itself. Your present psychosocial state can also act as a serious block to listening. I remember feeling bitter and angry over the death of someone I had dearly loved and carrying that psychosocial state into company. I was not in any place to listen to or empathise with others and, thankfully, a good friend suggested I would be better off being on my own and not inflicting myself on others. He was right. What I needed was to listen to myself and work through my grieving process.

Listening is essential to effective communication in the family. The presence of active listening will certainly ease the pressure in many situations, but be sure you do not slip into 'shoulds' and 'ought to's' or 'have to's' or advice-giving.

ADDICTION TO CARING

Love is a two-sided coin: it is about both the giving and the receiving of love. In general, women tend to be very good at giving love but poor at receiving it; on the other hand, men are masters at receiving love but novices at giving it. Hence women, who are the 'givers', go into the professions that demand the ability to nurture others (nursing, teaching, parenting, counselling, social work), and men, who have been reared to be the 'takers', go into the professions that are concrete, logical and non-emotionally demanding (science, legal, construction, business).

What is sad is that men have locked inside themselves the need to give love, and women have imprisoned their innate need to receive love. For men to risk showing love, and for women to risk receiving love, means going against the culture that still defines very polarised roles for men and women. When the polarisation is extreme, women become addicted to giving and men to taking. However, effective relationships are about 'give and take' and this two-way street ensures that the needs of both parties in a relationship are voiced and more often than not met.

The woman who has a compulsive drive to care for others rarely considers herself. She tends to be more concerned about helping others and never expects anything in return. Indeed, any attempt to give to a person who is locked into caring will be countered by embarrassment, protests of 'don't be wasting your money on me' or 'you shouldn't have done that' or 'haven't you enough to be thinking of'. Even more revealing is the attempt to block somebody who compulsively cares from doing things for others. Indeed, it is often more difficult to take a caring behaviour away from such a person than it is to take a drink or drug away from someone who is addicted to alcohol or drugs. The response to 'I can manage by myself' will be met by sulking or withdrawal or 'you don't want me in your life'. Very often 'for peace sake', the partner will give in and allow the caring to continue; this reaction is neither good for him nor for the person who is driven to care. It means the addictive cycle will continue and the relationship remains one-sided for both parties – she to give and he to take.

Not surprisingly, relationships that are one-way will eventually break down. The person who is driven to care is often overwhelmed when a partner or son or daughter attempts to break away. She feels 'how could they do this after all I've done for them'. Sadly, what she does not realise is that constant doing for another renders the receiver helpless and, most importantly, blocks him (or her) from the privilege of exhibiting love. Helping is not about doings things for others; rather it is about giving people skills so that they can do things for themselves. What people addicted to caring often fail to see is that their kind of helping is profoundly arrogant, because in effect what they are saying is 'I know what's best for you'. People who are addicted to caring find it extremely difficult to let others be free to make their own decisions and mistakes. Most of all, they make it difficult for others to demonstrate love.

Women and men who are addicted to helping others subconsciously believe that if they are always helpful, others will need them and therefore like them more. They do not have a sense that they are worthy to receive love (only to give it), and so they undervalue themselves and allow themselves to be taken advantage of.

The turning point that is required is a recognition of the addictive pattern, the development of a sense of self that is deserving of both the giving and receiving of love, a valuing of one's own needs and the creation of a balance between giving and receiving. As with all addictions, help, support and patience is needed to reach a state of well-being.

THE POWER OF ANGER

Next to the welfare feeling of love, the emergency feeling of anger is the most important feeling that helps us to move forward in life. Anger is well termed as an 'emergency' feeling, because it alerts you to the presence of some threat to your well-being and your need to take corrective action. Many people have major difficulties in either expressing or over-expressing anger. The former are fearful and the latter are forceful in that they attempt to control others (rather than self) through anger. Those who suppress their anger employ passivity and people-pleasing to appease their own or another's anger. Because they do not use the energy of anger to express their needs, beliefs, worthiness and grievances, their growth remains static. Equally, those who express their anger through verbal or physical aggression do not move forward and remain stuck in a vicious cycle of insecurity. Many people, including professionals, confuse anger with aggression. Anger is a feeling and cannot hurt anyone; aggression is an action (verbal, physical, written) and can be seriously threatening to the security of others.

I recall one client who complained of abdominal pain. When I asked her if she expressed anger, she replied: 'Yes, all the time, I'm aggressive at work and I frequently fly off the handle at home.' When I asked her if she expressed anger towards her mother, she replied, 'Oh no, it would really upset her. And yet it is she that causes me to feel angry. So instead I take it out on everybody else'. In this woman's case her mother was not in a mature place to understand a sudden onslaught of anger directed towards her, but the truth behind this daughter-mother situation was that it was the daughter who had to change, not the mother. The woman described her mother as 'perfectionistic', 'fussy' and 'for whom you could do nothing right'. And yet the daughter continued to visit her mother with the subconscious hope that sometime she would receive approval and hence love from her mother. 'She makes me so angry,' she complained. But I pointed out to her that it is more appropriate to say that 'I feel angry at myself for allowing her to rule my life'.

Anger is the fire of the emotions; it is the power that will help us to move forward. Anger says, 'You must do something about this untenable situation.' In this woman's case she saw that her dependence on approval from her mother needed to be outgrown and that she was now an adult who could approve and love herself. As the woman internalised and lived out this awareness, her attitude towards her mother gradually changed. She began to see that her mother had no sense of her own worthiness and therefore found it difficult to approve others. As the daughter's feelings of self-worth grew, her stomach pains disappeared and she was able to give praise and affection to her own children and spouse, and also to her mother. The latter dynamic eased the hostility between them. It is important that the emergency of anger is turned into something creative that can be used for personal growth.

Other experiences of threatening expressions of anger are seen when a husband shouts at his wife who is sick in bed, for example. Nine times out of ten, the source of the husband's anger is fear. He is dependent on his wife and relies on her to be strong — he cannot bear the idea that he may have to cope alone. It is not uncommon for such husbands to die before their wives, even though their wives may have become seriously ill before them. It is still a sad situation that the socialisation of male children leads them to hide their true feelings rather than expressing their fears and anxieties.

Expression of all feelings, including anger, must start with the words 'I feel . . .' and not 'You make me . . .' When you own your feelings, you are likely to see the opportunities for growth that they present. Nobody can make you do anything. In the end, whether consciously or subconsciously, the decision is yours.

BEYOND FORGIVENESS

I do not believe in forgiveness. Forgiveness implies superiority and judgment, and does more harm than good. When I say to you 'I forgive you for being violent', I show no under-standing of why you engaged in a threatening behaviour and I act like a benign judge by extending the hand of forgiveness. The judgment in this case has been on your 'bad' behaviour and I am forgiving you for being violent. But people are not their behaviour and the confusion of behaviour with person creates major insecurity.

I have always been impressed by Jesus' words to the woman taken in adultery: 'Has no one judged you?' She replied, 'No Lord'. And Jesus said: 'Neither will I, go in peace and sin no more.' What Jesus did not do was ask why the woman had got involved with another man. Maybe many of her needs were not being met in her marriage relationship and the extra-marital relationship filled the void created by the unmet needs. Maybe the woman had a subconscious drive to find accept-ance from men, because the first man in her life (her father) had badly rejected her. There are many possibilities. The important issue here is that people do not deliberately perpe-trate neglect, but from some hurt place inside themselves they engage in actions that are designed to reduce future threats to their emotional or sexual or social or spiritual well-being.

I recently worked with a parent who was constantly critical of his sixteen-year-old son and had been for years. The boy's mother paid him scant attention. The boy cleverly avoids the company of all adults, has nervous tics and seeks out in a dominating but clinging way the company of peers. The boy feels unloved by his mother and father and at some point in his life he will need to come to terms with this sad experience. Helping him to do that will mean exposing the vulnerability of his father and mother. His father is highly dependent on the approval of others and wanted his son to be perfect so that he would gain acceptance. His dependence has crippled both his son and his son's development. This dependence was his legacy from his own childhood. The boy's mother is work addicted and attempts to find her recognition through work performance. Until each parent resolves the rejection of self and enmeshment with others and work, they will not be able to correct their relationship with their son. What their son needs to show his parents is not forgiveness, but com-passion. They have not deliberately hurt him (which is what forgiveness suggests), and they, like him, require healing of their hidden selves. In the embrace of compassion both parents and son can find the light of unconditional love and understanding of each other.

The notion of forgiveness has been an integral part of our Catholic culture. From an early age, we were taught that we were 'sinners' who needed forgiveness and that God had to send his son Jesus to suffer intolerable pain to redeem us; this belief has neither been Christian nor psychologically empowering. Jesus showed the way to unconditional love; he neither judged nor condemned. The Catholic blaming approach infected the majority and became generalised to all behaviours that are offensive. I work with many people who say: 'I will never be able to forgive my father (or mother or partner or friend or bombers) for what they have done.' I understand that their unforgiving behaviour is there to protect them from further hurt. Forgiveness means reaching out to those who have been a source of threat, but when you are not ready and safe it is not wise to do it.

Forgiveness and compassion are hard-won. People who have been violated need safety to express their horror, anger, fear, hate and despair and to again feel secure before they reach out to those who violated them. However, even when you come to a place of forgiveness, I believe there is a further road to be travelled, on which you will meet the milestones of unconditional love and understanding that people who hurt act out from hurt places. I recently shared a conference platform with a high court judge, and I was impressed when he said that he is patently and painfully aware that when he sentences a person for a crime, that person has also been a victim of neglect. I am not at all suggesting that people must not be responsible for their actions, but such responsibility is only likely to emerge where compassion and understanding abound. Responsibility is both an individual and collective issue. Where there is judgment, pressure to conform, rejection, threat, dismissal and forgiveness, there is no collective responsibility to make it emotionally, socially and physically safe for individuals to resolve the reasons why they are alienated. The high recidivist rate (minimum 80 per cent) of people who commit crimes is indicative of such attitudes. Hopefully, the current emergence of a pluralist society may give rise to a new order that is both spiritually and psychosocially sound.

LIVING FROM YOUR HEAD

Many people, men in particular, always start the conversation with 'I think' rather than 'I feel'. They answer questions clearly and precisely, although they never mention a feeling. They are comfortable with logic and fact and may ridicule or look down on those who are 'over-emotional'. Such emotional illiteracy has its roots in early childhood:

□ Aggression and violence in the home may lead to children suppressing their feelings.
□ The non-expression of feelings by parents may be imitated by the children.
□ Children's expressed feelings may be verbally or physically suppressed.

For example:

□ 'Don't cry — it gives Mummy a headache.'
□ 'Don't cry/be angry — you know it upsets me and your father.'
□ 'Please make Mummy happy and be quiet.'
□ 'You don't care that your behaviour upsets me.'

These examples are emotional blackmail and can rule someone's life for a long time, even a lifetime. Often when you ask those who suppress their feelings to describe what makes them angry, they will answer, 'Nothing'.

Adults who suppress their feelings are often the peace-makers; they avoid conflict where possible. They are the 'listeners', everybody tells them their problems but they rarely express their own. They may feel resentful and hurt, but they do not complain as there is often a fear of releasing their anger in case they cannot control it. Also the old fear of how others will react to their expression of feelings maintains the suppression. In physical terms, this resentment and anger becomes buried in the liver area, and in acupuncture terms it creates problems along the liver meridian. In other cases, crying may have been suppressed because it was seen as a sign of weakness. The message was to 'be strong', 'put on a brave face', and the child had to learn prematurely to be independent and brave.

I recall a priest in his fifties who came to me for help because no matter what sad or tragic situation he encountered he could not cry. He had worked in Third World countries ravaged by wars, famine, floods, political exploitation and earth-quakes. He had seen babies alive in their dead mothers' arms, bodies torn apart by violence, untold butchery – and yet he could not cry. When he was two years of age, his mother had beaten him for two hours until he stopped crying. He cleverly learned to suppress any hint of expression of upset.

Restrained tears appear in the physical body as excess fluid, such as catarrh which drips down the back of the throat, or swelling of the extremities. The general rule is that which is not expressed externally will need to be expressed internally. Therefore, suppressed emotions often manifest as psycho-somatic conditions:

- skin rashes (unexpressed irritation)
- asthma (unexpressed speech)
- diarrhoea (unexpressed fear)
- fat intolerance (unexpressed anger)

Conditions such as the above verify that many ailments reflect an underlying emotional obstruction to the flow of life. When expressed appropriately, crying and anger are natural releases of energy – both are part of the grieving or aggrieving process which aid the person to 'let go' of a situation that has been completed and to make room for new experiences. Once there is awareness of the suppressed emotion, then this can be gently but consciously released without requiring physical illness, external changes or a cathartic experience. Blocked emotions can lead to disease; awareness leads to freedom.

Women tend to be much more expressive of their feelings — except anger. However, in the last two decades more and more women have learned to assert (anger expression) their presence, at least in the Western world. It is a fact that women outlive men by an average of eight to ten years, and this is due in no small way to their greater emotional literacy. Men dearly need to take on the challenge of emotional expression. Feelings are the most accurate barometer of each person's reality. You can play games in your head but you cannot fool your heart.

MEN IN CRISIS

Men are required less and less as providers or protectors by women. It is becoming commonplace for women to choose to live without men, and fatherhood is threatened by in vitro fertilisation, donor semination and cloning.

Only a small percentage of men attend lectures and courses on personal development, relationships, self-worth, family development and communication. Neither do the majority of men go to parent-teacher meetings, seek out help to resolve personal, family, marital or work difficulties, or show ease around the expression of love, fear, sadness, grief, loneliness and depression.

Men die on average eight years before women, and Irish men are seven times more likely to actually commit suicide, whereas Irish women are ten times more likely to attempt it. In most areas of the country, 30 to 40 per cent of babies are born to single mothers. Furthermore, when a marriage ends in separation or divorce, in over 90 per cent of cases the mothers are the ones left holding the babies. Curiously, it is women who are tending to blow the whistle on unhappy marital relationships. However, when it comes to creating second relationships, the percentages are reversed: 90 per cent of men, compared to 10 per cent of women, enter a long-term relationship within one year of the break-up of their marriage. The worrying issue is whether or not men reflect on the reasons for the failure of their marriage, so that they give more mature consideration to the formation of a new relationship.

Work addiction is more common among men than women. Also, aggression is still the most frequent reaction of men under pressure. In terms of career options, men continue to avoid professions that demand nurturing characteristics, such as nursing, teaching, parenting, social work, clinical psychology and counselling.

There is no doubt that men have all sorts of problems, some of them unique to their gender. However, whilst women have made some strides towards emancipation over the last two decades, they too can be credited with a list of problems, some of them peculiar to their sex – passivity, addiction to caring, definition of self through the other, dependence on physicality, difficulties in the expression of anger, lack of self-care and receptivity to affirmation. Furthermore, women are more prone to depression than men, smoke more than men and get drunk as much as men. Married career women with children are the most at risk health group.

What is often not emphasised when people or professionals talk about men or women in crisis is that these gender problems are due to a socialisation process that has determined very different roles for men and women. It is not gender problems we need to be talking about but social problems. There has been a subconscious collusion between men and women that has brought about the challenges that face both sexes. Change will only occur when men and women work separately and together to free each other of their stereotypical prisons. Men need to work inwards and women outwards, but such movements are only made possible by cooperation between the sexes. Inward movement has to do with the realm of feelings, intimacy, nurturance and self-worth, and outward movement has to do with the world of expansiveness of vision, assertiveness, legitimate power, drive and entrepreneurship.

The social systems (home, school, workplace, church, community, country) that men and women inhabit need to change so that both sexes have opportunities to develop and express inwardness and outwardness. Irish society has been largely patriarchal, and this has not been beneficial to either men or women. Our culture needs to become humanistic and expansive in vision for all its members and move away from the polarisation of males and females.

DO MOTHERS-IN-LAW RUIN MARRIAGES?

Mothers-in-law have long been the target of comedians, but is there any truth in the jests? A new book, *Mothers-in-law are seriously dangerous to your health*, written by a Spanish psychologist and lawyer, states that conflict with mothers-in-law is one of the most often-cited causes of divorce in Spain. Indeed, it would appear that much strife among couples in all countries is caused by mothers-in-law, and letters about such conflicts often dominate agony aunt columns. Typical complaints from daughters-in-law are that mothers-in-law dominate and interfere, treat them like slaves and refuse to let go of their sons. They also claim that mothers-in-law have no life outside their sons.

Of course, the source of the difficulties between mothers-in-law and daughters-in-law is the immature relationship that exists between the mothers and their sons. Unfortunately, this more often than not gets acted out between the two women in the man's life. There is no doubt that the son remains dependent on his mother and probably becomes confused when conflict breaks out between his partner and his mother. There is the added confounding factor that sons tend to marry their mothers, or the opposite of their mothers. More typically, they marry a woman similar to their mother, and the emotional triangle between the three protagonists can involve a high degree of tension, with the two women viewing each other as competitors. Consequently, the man is caught in the dilemma of conflicting loyalties. However, it needs to be seen that he was entrapped before the marriage and now finds himself landed with a double entrapment.

Triangulation inevitably results in the third party (in this case, the daughter-in-law) being in the most vulnerable situation. If she complains to her partner about his mother, she risks his aggression or withdrawal from her. Indeed, male partners often distance themselves from the unhappy situation, leaving their partners feeling neglected and angry. If the wife takes the issue directly to her mother-in-law, she risks her wrath and her complaining about her to her son. Ironically, the two people who really need to sort out their relationship – mother and son – are left off the hook in this relationship triangle.

The wisest approach the daughter-in-law can take is to keep the relationship with her partner separate from her relationship with her mother-in-law. She needs to be very definite in the expression of her fair needs to her partner and be quite assertive when any pattern of neglect arises due to demands from her mother-in-law. However, rather than complaining about his mother – which is not the real issue – she must assert her needs within the couple relationship, as it is the non-meeting of these needs that is the real issue for her. When her partner complains that he cannot say no to his mother, or that he feels responsible for her (even though she is quite healthy), she needs to say definitely, but supportively, that he needs to sort that issue out for himself. In this way she does not create a triangle.

But what about the situation when, in spite of asserting her needs and requesting directly that her partner sorts out his co-dependent relationship with his mother, he favours his mother and neglects her needs? There are two issues that require consideration here. The first is that the wife does not repeat the pattern of a co-dependent relationship with her husband. There is no possibility of resolution when this happens. She must be determined to show that she is not dependent, and that she can stand on her own two capable feet. The second issue is that actions always speak louder than words, and with this in mind she must follow through in getting her unmet needs met herself. After all, the independent person takes responsibility for her own needs, and the expression of needs in a relationship is not a command, but a request. Incidentally, such a modelling of self-reliance and independence may be the key support that the woman's partner needs to establish an adult to adult relationship with his mother.

When it comes to interactions with her mother-in-law, the wife must be interiorily very clear where the boundaries lie around the couple relationship, herself, and, where there are children, the rearing of the children. As with her husband, she needs to follow through in word and action the maintenance of these boundaries. With such clarity she will have no need to be aggressive or manipulative, and it is quite possible that her mother-in-law will recognise and accept such maturity. When she doesn't, no argument is required, only definite action.

When a son marries a woman who is opposite in personality to his mother, the danger is that his wife will be passive in the face of her mother-in-law's interference, and it may be further down the years of her marriage before she sees the untenable situation. When she does, it is the first step towards emancipation.

Finally, I do know of very supportive relationships that exist between mothers-in-law and daughters-in-law, and much can be learned from these mature relationships by women who are in conflict with one another.

SEPARATED BUT NOT GONE

The rising tide of marital separation and divorce does not mean that the rate of marital disharmony has increased. What it does point to is that individuals are not prepared to put up with continual non-meeting of their needs. My own belief is that separation and divorce should be the last resort and that the couple deserve to pursue sincere and genuine attempts to resolve their differences, either between themselves or with the help of an unbiased third party. Resolution may mean either an enhancement of the marital relationship or an amicable parting. However, what is more common is that either the couple or one partner refuses to talk or go for help and the relationship ends in considerable turmoil, with the result that so much of what needs to get spoken about remains hidden and manifests itself in bitterness, resentment, disillusionment, hate and blame. Such unfinished business means that, although the couple may have physically separated, they are still unhealthily bound up emotionally, socially and financially with each other. Where there are children, this continuation of the couple conflict plays havoc with family welfare. Marital conflict does not have to lead to family conflict but, regrettably, nine times out of ten it does.

Separated couples have a duty to each other and to their children to resolve their differences, so that as individuals they can freely progress in maturity and as parents they can support each other to maintain family harmony.

The partner who remains enmeshed can exhibit a range of possessive, dependent and difficult behaviours:

- ☐ frequently calling to the house
- ☐ constantly calling on the mobile phone
- ☐ turning up at social events where partner is likely to be
- ☐ complaining to children about partner
- ☐ getting over-emotional and making an utter spectacle of self
- ☐ using maintenance money as a weapon
- ☐ expecting ex-partner to continue to take care of him (or her)
- ☐ following ex-partner to social events
- ☐ driving past the house frequently
- ☐ phoning and putting the phone down when answered
- ☐ phoning partner for help with a blocked drain or a car that won't start

Just as for those who perpetuate these actions, partners who allow the above intrusions into their private lives have not separated out, and it is the mutual enmeshment of the separated couple that maintains the unhappy situation. For example, women who call on their ex-partners to fix the car, mow the lawn or paint the house are secretly pleased that they still have some level of control, as they have not yet come to a place of believing that they can cope on their own. Similarly, men who claim to be outraged by their ex-partner's continual checking of their movements are covertly pleased. It feeds their egos and gives them a sexual safety net. I know of men who, following a falling out with a mistress, within hours would be knocking at their ex-partner's door for comfort.

There can be more serious violations of privacy following separation – stalking, major verbal aggression, violence and uninvited visits, using children as pawns in the conflict, turning children against a parent and public humiliation of a partner. Such actions are evidence of deep insecurity, low self-worth and incredible dependence. No matter what the source is, partners under siege must not tolerate such invasiveness; they must establish strong boundaries and, when necessary, secure a protection order. The purpose of this order is not to punish; it is there to safeguard the rights of the victim:

- the right to privacy
- the right to freedom
- the right to safety from sexual, physical, emotional and social violations
- the right to respect

Separated men or women who do not stand up for their rights are in need of as much help to access their own dignity, power and independence as those who perpetrate overt violations.

THE VIOLENCE OF SILENCE

There are marriages in which one partner has not spoken a word to the other partner for several years. For example, the husband may have cut off communication with his wife due to her not agreeing with his religious or moral views or not meeting particular emotional or sexual needs. This silence cuts deeply into the self-esteem of the wife, leaving her feeling helpless, unworthy and disempowered. Where there are children or financial and emotional dependence, the wife may find that her only option is to 'give in' to the unrealistic demands and restore some semblance of normality to the relationship. By doing this she does violence to herself and to her children, as she has sacrificed her own beliefs and needs, and models yielding to emotional blackmail. These responses are ones that her children may repeat in their relationship with their father and others. This besieged mother needs help and strong support to come to a place of holding onto her own deep regard for herself, her beliefs and her rights for equality and respect in this relationship. The partner who uses the 'silent treatment' also needs help to become independent, respectful and loving of self and partner.

Silence can also be used as a weapon by parents to get children to conform to their ways. Some young adults relay stories of mothers (or fathers) not talking to them because they disagree with their choice of friend, or lover, or life-partner or career. These parents are seeking through sulking and withdrawing to get their children to live their lives according to their own principles and needs. This does serious violence to the rights of their children to make their own life choices, choose their own friends and find their own meaning in life. Young adults who 'give in' to such parents will have deep hidden resentment and anger and are unlikely to become self-fulfilled in life. How could they when they are living the lives of their parents and not being true to themselves? In this context, Shakespeare's 'to thine own self be true' speaks volumes.

Another type of silence that perpetuates violence is passivity. Passivity turns a blind eye to the ills of family, marital and work relationships. There are parents who passively accept verbal, physical, emotional and even sexual violations of themselves and their children. It is a sad indictment of our society that one in five women are subject to physical violence and that at least 20 per cent of employees suffer serious verbal aggression. There is also a sizeable percentage of men who are subjected to physical and verbal violence by their female partners. Silence on and passivity to such violations reinforce these neglectful behaviours.

The typical signs of passivity are over-pleasing others, timidity, shyness, fearfulness, non-assertiveness, avoidance of conflict and conformity. Passivity means that the needs of people who are passive are not voiced or met; neither are the needs of others in their charge (children, students, employees) ensured.

It is not that people who are passive or use the 'silent treatment' want to deliberately hurt or let themselves or others down. Passivity is employed to protect from hurt and rejection. It protects because it seeks to control an aggressor by giving in all or some of the time. If you are passive, you ingeniously protect yourself from hurt and rejection by never going up against others. 'Silent treatment' is also aimed at controlling other people's behaviour, particularly behaviours that threaten your self-image. By getting others to conform to your ways, you offset their judgments of you. However, whether you are being protectively passive or protectively manipulative, you do violence to both yourself and others. When it is the former, your passivity neglects yourself and others and maintains dysfunctional relationships and self-worth difficulties. When it is the latter, your manipulative 'silent' behaviour blocks the development of the person whose behaviour threatens you, it damages the relationship and perpetuates personal insecurities and interpersonal neglect.

Speaking out on silent violence and, indeed, on overt violence, is an essential step to resolving the cause of such protective tactics. Equally, the empowering of those who employ the protective weapon of passivity is central to the resolution of many relationship difficulties. Breaking the silence does not imply that you are blowing the whistle on someone, nor that you are being an informant. Regrettably, many children feel that speaking out about being bullied, overtly or covertly, by peers or adults is a weakness. Unfortunately, those who do speak out often find that their revelations fall on deaf ears, and they learn that it is safer to say nothing. Sometimes these children may be listened to but no action is taken with regard to their complaints, and this is as punishing as non-listening.

Both adults and children need to be given strong and frequent permission to voice blocks to their happiness; whether these take the form of 'silent treatment' or aggressive control. It is essential that actions follow revelations. The most important people to talk to are those who will listen, lend support and help you to take appropriate actions on violations to your good sense of self. Sometimes the mere breaking of silence brings about change.

Voicing neglect is not only an act of caring by victims of themselves, it is also caring of the perpetrators of the difficult behaviours. The caring for self is expressed by the assertion that 'I am somebody of worth and I deserve caring and respect'. The caring for the perpetrator in confrontation is: 'I regard you as somebody of worth and I respect you enough to let you know that these behaviours are intolerable to me.' Change is now possible for all, and the relationship between the victim and the perpetrator is now open for improvement. Everybody loses out when silence is maintained.

THE END OF MARRIAGE!

In a recent *Sunday Times* interview, Anthony Clare, psychiatrist and author of *On Men: Masculinity in Crisis*, stated: 'If I had the power I would abolish marriage. I would establish the major moment as the decision to have a child. That is when you want two people to pledge something to each other, and that is what we should acknowledge with a big ceremony. The wedding ceremony means nothing any more.'

Whilst I agree that the decision to create a family needs to be more marked by ritual than it is, I think Professor Clare is confusing two distinct relationships. A child is a sacred creation and requires the commitment of both father and mother to his or her physical, emotional, social, sexual, intellectual, educational, creative and spiritual development. No easy responsibility this! Too many young people, both couples and singles, take on the responsibility too lightly. In my view, parenting needs to be seen as a paid profession, and not only do parents need to formally celebrate their decision to have a child, but the State should also have structures in place that require formal registration of and training for parenting. It is fascinating to observe the standards that operate in Irish society whereby we are required to have a licence for a television, a test for driving a car, but there are no criteria laid down for the momentous act of bringing another human being into this world.

The pledge that parents need to make towards their newborn child is an essentially different commitment to their marriage to each other. After all, what children require of parents is to bring them to a place of emotional, social, spiritual, intellectual and financial independence so that they can eventually leave the nest. Parenting is effectively about letting go, even from children's earliest years. When parents do not have a good commitment to each other, they frequently transfer their unmet needs to their children. This results in an enmeshed relationship that can stifle a child's development. Children need to be given over to life, not to parents.

A marriage pledge, on the other hand, is not about letting go; it is more about setting up a life-long relationship. It involves a special mutual dedication of love, support, understanding, encouragement for each other's individual emotional, social, career and spiritual development and the development of a life together. It is where each appoints the other the guardian of their solitude and their intimacy with each other. There is equality, fairness, sharing, friendship, sexual intimacy, interest in each other's lives, creation of a home and being there for each other. Marriage is a declaration of this commitment.

It is the marriage relationship that needs to be the bedrock of family life. Too many people decide to have children to strengthen an ailing marriage, but this rarely works and the fallout for all concerned can be serious. Children are more likely to get the best possible care from a couple who provide each other with mutual care. Rather than abolish marriage, what is required is an education that prepares people for this all-important, life-long relationship. The rapid rise in the number of people living together before marriage, along with the rise in separation and divorce, are not reasons to abolish marriage but must act as a spur to reinstate the importance and sacredness of the marriage relationship.

Finally, there is a high percentage of couples who are choosing not to have children but who see that their 'major moment' is their life-long pledge to each other, which they wish to celebrate with a 'big ceremony'.

In so many ways the marriage pledge and the pledge to have children are separate commitments and it is best not to enmesh them.

WHAT MEN REALLY WANT

What do men think of the limited view that popular authors have of them in their advice to women on 'how to get your man' and 'what determines relationship success?' For example, Laura Doyle, author of the dreadfully titled *The Surrendered Wife*, and who is currently writing *The Surrendered Single*, advises single women:

- Let him ask all the questions.
- Talk about his interests.
- Let him reveal what he wants to . . . don't press him.
- If he offers you a compliment, accept it graciously.
- Don't try to change him.
- List the traits you like in him.
- Never ask him out.
- Bite your tongue even when you strongly disagree with him.
- Don't list your achievements, you will make him feel inferior.
- To get a second date, offer him your telephone number.
- Think: 'There is no such thing as a perfect man, but there are lots of imperfect men to have a wonderful relationship with.'

As a man, my first reaction to the above list is to suggest that women should to run a mile from any man who would want them to conform to this list – it is a recipe for personal invisibility and relationship conflict. My second response is that, while I agree that it is not a good idea to attempt to control or change me, I am certainly not somebody who is so hypersensitive that you need to tiptoe around me. I would want a female partner, lover or friend to be herself, to feel that we need to be equally there for each other and that both of us can be expressive of what we think and feel. To suggest that a woman's achievements, interests, opinions and beliefs are a source of threat is gross arrogance and superiority. Surely, relationships depend on people being *real* with each other; to suggest that a woman puts on a false persona to 'keep her man' is insulting to both men and women.

Vanessa Lloyd Platt, the London divorce lawyer who wrote *Secrets of Relationship Success*, blamed women for the ever-increasing British divorce rate. She wrote that 'endless studies have shown that men are not built to cope with women's complaints about work. They simply are not designed to absorb women's pressures as well as their own.' She goes on to say that women, by contrast, possess the ability to spread their coping mechanisms to encompass their male partners. The latter seems to imply that men still require 'mother figures' to look after them. Furthermore, when Lloyd Platt suggests a 'design flaw' in men, is she thinking the source of this is nurture or nature? Surely if one half of the adult population believes that the other half is incapable of emotional reciprocity, why would men bother to prove the opposite? Lloyd Platt strongly asserts that 'men just can't expand their psychological profile to adapt to the changes in relationships and family that contemporary society has wrought'. Are these the same men who have travelled to outer space, who are technological wizards, scientific explorers, artists, poets, writers, conservationists, lovers, fathers, chefs, horticulturists . . .! Why is it that some women authors, sociologists and psychologists doubt men's capacity to develop the full breadth of human qualities?

Maybe, maybe, there is a projection going on – that it is women who are afraid of men developing their feminine side!

My own belief is that, with support within and across gender, both men and women have limitless potential to become fully human. There is no doubt that women have had the advantage of the 'feminist' (better title – 'masculinist') movement over the last twenty years. But such advantage cannot be allowed to cloud the fact that men possess the same power to expand their psychological profile. In my own practice and in personal development courses, I daily witness men doing just that.

I believe that many men would welcome women relating to them in the following ways:

☐ Be real.
☐ Express your needs, feelings and beliefs, and allow men to do likewise.
☐ Do not be intrusive or invasive – allow men to be free to be themselves.
☐ Trust that men can take care of themselves.
☐ Believe that men are capable of full human expression.
☐ Say 'no' or 'yes' when you want to.
☐ Take the initiative when you want to.
☐ Make requests, not demands.
☐ See that difference and disagreement are critical to a healthy relationships, once mutual respect is present.
☐ Be supportive in times of crisis.
☐ Think: 'Intimacy is where two individuals love and value each other and where each appoints the other the guardian of their solitude.'

SAVING MARRIAGE

New research suggests that one in five young people will never marry, and the likelihood is that this ratio will increase. There is no doubt that everyone wants to love and be loved, but somehow marriage is becoming a less attractive option for meeting that primary need. The indications are that living together is more desirable, but more than one third of such liaisons end in less than ten years. Presently, that figure is significantly greater than the level of marital breakdown. It would appear that cohabitation is no more successful than marriage in sustaining intimacy. Furthermore, of those who cohabit, only three-fifths marry, even though three-quarters would have planned to marry.

Many long-term married couples may be appalled by these figures, but it must be realised that an intact marriage does not necessarily mean a happy and fulfilling one. While a life-long commitment would seem to offer the solidity and safety that many young people crave, many young people have witnessed the collapse of their parents' marriages, so why would they believe they would be any more successful? There are other possible reasons why matrimony is in decline:

- ◻ Women, in particular, want more from life than kitchen, church, bedroom.
- ◻ There is a higher level of education and career opportunities for women.
- ◻ Young people are seeing divorce as the end point of marriage.
- ◻ Living together is less binding.

- ☐ There is greater societal acceptance of cohabitation.
- ☐ There are no songs, films, novels about ongoing marriages, except to examine their failure. The same can be said about families.

When children enter the equation, the evidence is that nothing compares to a stable marriage in terms of the well-being of children. Nevertheless, the presence of children does not create stability; indeed children are less and less seen as a reason for a couple to stay together. The decision to have children needs to be made on the bedrock of a couple's strong commitment to each other; children are not the cement that holds a couple together.

There is no question that when it comes to intimacy, marriage is the most difficult decision of them all, and that is how it needs to be seen. In the past, too many starry-eyed lovers entered the married state without due consideration of what a life-long commitment entails. My own belief is that such a commitment offers the most powerful and solid forum for two people to continue to develop as individuals and as a couple. Until recently, one of the major weaknesses of marriage was that individuality and difference were seen as threats to intimacy, rather than its cornerstone. As soon as oppressed married people were free of religious threat and family censure, they escaped to find someone who would see and love them for their unique selves.

Marriage needs to be presented to young people as an intimate relationship in which:

- ☐ a life-long commitment is about giving and receiving
- ☐ separateness is the basis for togetherness
- ☐ each partner loves, touches and respects the other and appoints the other the guardian of their solitude

- individuality is central to intimacy
- autonomy is the foundation of monogamy
- a solid and safe place for life-long intimacy and friendship is created
- a life-long commitment is seen as a dynamic and glamorous life option

An open and honest discussion on the true nature of marriage needs to occur to prevent contemporary Ireland from sliding down into high marital and relationship breakdown and major instability in families. Education and preparation of young people for relationships needs to become an important part of school, home, community, government and church agendas. Most of all, adults need to model a way of relating to others that is balanced, mature, non-possessive and enduring. Change does not start with children but with adults.

PART TWO
FAMILY

- ☐ Love is more than showing affection
- ☐ Intuitive parenting
- ☐ Children 'out of control' – a parent's nightmare
- ☐ The reality of family life
- ☐ Children in distress
- ☐ Adolescents in hiding
- ☐ Teenage rebellion
- ☐ Women hit too!
- ☐ Mothers under fire again
- ☐ Boys will be girls!
- ☐ Premature leave-taking
- ☐ The decline of the family
- ☐ Letting go is hard to do
- ☐ Parents who reflect are more effective

LOVE IS MORE THAN SHOWING AFFECTION

There is only one kind of love and that is unconditional love. Unconditional love corresponds to the deepest longing not only of children but of every adult. However, such non-possessive warmth is rare.

When we say we have been loving, it is important to check what we mean by such a declaration. Many parents who bring distressed children and adolescents for help claim angrily that 'we have done everything for them'. But this can be a protective illusion, because in reality these parents, albeit unwittingly, have been cross, irritable, judgmental or have projected their own needs and ways onto their children or have been addicted to work or perfectionism or have deep fears of failure and rejection and are highly concerned with how other people view them. Some of these parents may still remain unhealthily enmeshed with their family of origin, to the detriment of their own marriages and nuclear families. Parents can only love children to the extent that they love themselves. Those in the helping professions can only bring their clients to the same level of development they have reached themselves. Whether parent or psychologist, none of us can avoid bringing some unresolved emotional baggage into our respective roles, and this inevitably limits the expansiveness of the love and care that children need for their holistic development.

It is possible to evaluate loving in terms of either 'what not to do' or 'what to do'. Unconditional love ceases when any of the following 'what not to do's' is contravened.

- ☐ Do not be cross.
- ☐ Do not be irritable.
- ☐ Do not label children.
- ☐ Do not withdraw affection because of a misdemeanour.
- ☐ Do not punish failure.
- ☐ Do not over-reward success.
- ☐ Do not project your own life or unmet needs onto children.
- ☐ Do not hit.
- ☐ Do not shout.
- ☐ Do not push.
- ☐ Do not compare.
- ☐ Do not confuse a child's behaviour with a child's sacred person.
- ☐ Do not over-protect.
- ☐ Do not spoil.
- ☐ Do not give in to unreasonable demands.
- ☐ Do not have unrealistic expectations.

The above list is by no means exhaustive. When parents or other significant adults in children's lives engage in behaviours contrary to the 'do nots', it is important to evaluate the frequency, intensity, endurance and duration of these unloving responses. We all lose control now and again, but when we genuinely apologise, the rift in the relationship is healed and harmony is restored. An excellent index of an unhappy family is wherein no one ever apologises.

Frequency is a measure of how often an unloving behaviour occurs; intensity has got to do with the severity of the unloving response; endurance is a measure of how long a particular blow to a child's self-worth lasts (a minute, five minutes, an hour, a day, etc.), and finally, duration is a measure of how long the neglectful behaviour has been going on – weeks, months, years. Clearly, the more frequent, intense, enduring and long-lasting the blocks, the more children are forced to hide their true selves behind massive defensive walls.

The love relationship is not only broken by the presence of ridicule, scolding, dismissiveness, physical punishment, etc., but also by the absence of warmth, listening, affection, understanding, tenderness, compassion, fun, support, encouragement and joy. Whilst no overt neglect may occur in some families, the absence of loving is an emotional desert that can dry up the well-spring of love that resides in every child's heart. There are children and adults who come for help who talk painfully about always feeling invisible. George Eliot's declaration: 'I like not only to be loved but to be told that I am loved, the realm of silence is large enough beyond the grave', is a wise admonition to us all.

In terms of the 'to do's', unconditional love is not only about non-possessive warmth, it also embraces:

- ☐ keeping person and behaviour separate
- ☐ affirmation of individuality
- ☐ celebration of difference
- ☐ active listening
- ☐ accepting that each child is unique
- ☐ belief in vast potential and giftedness
- ☐ allowing children to be free to be themselves
- ☐ fostering respect for others
- ☐ provision of opportunities for each child's unique development
- ☐ creation of definite relationship boundaries
- ☐ apologising when wrong
- ☐ helping children to retain their natural curiosity and eagerness to learn
- ☐ ensuring that all learning is positive

- □ standing up for children when their well-being is threatened (in home, school, community)
- □ understanding
- □ compassion
- □ patience
- □ positive firmness

Parenting involves a level of self-sacrifice that no other profession demands, and yet in spite of their best intentions some parents find themselves floundering in their caring of children. What these parents often fail to see is that all parenting starts with self, and it is the nature of our relationship with self that determines our relationship with our children.

INTUITIVE PARENTING

A new book, *Paranoid Parenting* by English sociologist Dr Frank Furedi, suggests that parenting is not a complex science; rather it is a normal and natural undertaking that involves a special relationship. Ironically, going against his own thesis, he advises parents not to listen to the so-called experts in human behaviour, but 'to trust their own instincts instead'. One wonders has Dr Furedi ever witnessed a totally distraught parent, who does not know how to cope with a child who is out of control or who refuses to come out of his room. The 'instinct' is often to take the child by the scruff of the neck and shake him into conformity – hardly a desirable parenting response.

I agree that parenting involves a special relationship. However, as adults will know, intimate relationships are complex in nature, not only because of the personal complexes each individual brings to the relationship, but also because of the competing needs of the individuals in the relationship. Furthermore, relationship difficulties between adults and between parents and children can often break down or become troubled due to subconscious defenses and outside social, economic and religious pressures. My own belief is that parents need all the help they can get and the professionalisation of parenting still needs to be a societal priority.

I am confused by Dr Furedi's use of the word 'instincts', because instincts in human beings have long been eroded by socialisation. Maybe what was meant was 'intuition', and indeed there is no more reliable barometer for parents to check out the wisdom of their parenting. The difficulty is that whilst children are highly intuitive, in contrast, adults have largely lost touch with their intuitive voices.

Intuition is perception beyond the five physical senses. It is that informational system which operates without data from the physical senses. It is part of your unconscious mind and it is there to guide you to pursue objectives that maximise your own and children's and other adults' development in this world.

Psychology has been slow to recognise intuition, except as a curiosity. The knowledge that is obtained through intuition has not generally been recognised and, therefore, this knowledge is not processed by the intellect. Nevertheless, so many people express regret about ignoring their 'gut' feelings on an issue.

Intuition is revealed in our hunches about danger, our 'gut' reactions, being drawn to a certain book, person, work; it is the sense that an idea that has never been tried before might work. It is the sudden answer to a question, the light that comes out of the confusion of darkness.

The guidance that parents or others receive through intuitive processes is as essential for their own and children's well-being and growth as sunshine and clean air. Of course it is true that answers that come through your intuitive process can often challenge what you would prefer to do. Also, the truth that comes through intuitive processes can be contaminated with your own fears. Here is a place to apply your intellect. In other words, you might think you are receiving a clear intuition, but if you examine it rationally, if you take it apart, you will be able to see that you are responding to an insecurity.

For example, parents intuitively believe that they need to hold their children's happiness at heart, but the way they interpret that truth often reveals insecurities. Slapping children 'for their own good' reveals a contaminated intuition. Closer scrutiny of the 'truth' can show a need for parents to control children so that they will not be seen by others as poor parents. Sometimes beatings can be a sub-conscious ploy by parents to ensure that their children achieve academically or artistically or athletically or otherwise, so that parents can live their lives through their children's achievements. It is in this sense that intuition can be blocked or contaminated by the emotional baggage that adults carry into their caring roles.

We can learn to develop and employ intuition, to ask for guidance and receive it. Just as there are ways to discipline the mind, such as logical thinking, studying, repetition, brainstorming, so, too, there are ways to engage and discipline the intuition. Resolving internal and external emotional conflicts by the end of each day is vital. Be sure you finish or at least make decisions on emotionally unfinished business before you go to bed — do not go to bed in anger, sadness or bitterness and do not take on the emotional issues of others. People can certainly do with support, but only the individuals themselves can resolve their own insecurities. The words of a Chinese sage encapsulate the recommendation for emotional tranquillity: 'There is nothing more powerful and creative than emptiness – from which men shrink.' Deep relaxation and meditation can help this process. A cleansing nutritional programme also aids intuition. A third requirement is the willingness to hear what your intuition says and act accordingly. Many people, for deep fear reasons, do not wish to hear what can be heard so easily, and, therefore, they deny that they hear anything.

A final recommendation is to develop the realisation that there is a reason for all that happens in our lives, and that reason, at its core, is always compassionate and good. This is an essential belief that needs to be in place in order to activate and cultivate intuition.

CHILDREN 'OUT OF CONTROL' – A PARENT'S NIGHTMARE

A not unfamiliar scenario is a parent not dealing effectively with a teenager or child who responds aggressively to a 'no' or a request to do something. Sometimes the young person's verbal aggression can spill over into violence towards a parent or self or destruction of property. Some children or adolescents can keep up the onslaught for a lengthy time. The more 'out-of-control' the aggression is, the more difficult it is to deal with the situation calmly and effectively. Parents can be certain of three things:

☐ The purpose of the aggressive response is for the perpetrator to control the parent in order for him (or her) to get his own way.
☐ Aggression is not an acceptable means for any member of the family to gain any favourable response to a need.
☐ Responding to aggression with aggression is guaranteed to escalate the 'out-of-control' situation.

In the first instance, the issue is emotionally weighted for the perpetrator, and that has triggered the emotional and/or physical storm. However, in the immediate situation, the perpetrator is in no place to hear reason and it is counter-productive to attempt to discuss or argue the 'hot' issue. The response needed is one that will defuse the situation, and very often that means saying nothing more and removing yourself from the perpetrator. After all, you have made your position clear or declared a particular need. To continue to protest your situation not only weakens the conviction of your position, but it provides the perpetrator with a chink in your armour. More often than not you will be pursued and the pressure will continue. But aggression is like a fire – feed it and it will blaze all the more; stop feeding it and it will extinguish. So when pursued, maintain your 'no response' stance and address yourself to tasks in hand.

Later on, when calm has been restored, it is advisable to inquire what led to such an unacceptable outburst. Do not assume that you know what is wrong with your son or daughter, but show concern about the level of upset they exhibited.

With regard to the second certainty listed above, there needs to be a very definite ground rule within the family that under no circumstances will aggression be tolerated as a means of interaction. What is accepted and encouraged is mutual respect and communication that is direct, clear and allows the receiver the freedom to say 'yes' or 'no' or 'I'll need to think about it'. Your child does deserve an explanation for a negative response.

The most powerful response to aggressive behaviour is to ensure that it does not achieve its end, which is control. Furthermore, because aggression violates the rights to respect and safety of parents and other siblings, some sanction needs to follow its manifestation. The purpose of the sanction is not to punish but to vindicate and restore the parent's violated rights. The sanctions can range from a request for an apology to a deprivation of a privilege, to reporting the violation to an authority figure. It is vital that the sanction is imposed in a way that is respectful, non-punishing and meaningful. For example, 'I am not accepting being pushed by you because I deserve respect and safety. I am going to report this matter to your father. My purpose in doing this is to ensure no further violations of my rights.'

In applying a sanction, it is mature to start with the least and, when necessary, work up to the most safeguarding of the sanctions. A sanction is only a sanction when it restores a violated right. Once the right is reinstated, no further reference to the aggressive action needs to be made. Some parents keep bringing up, like a broken record, incidences of aggression. Such threatening behaviour is bound to produce another hostile response.

The third certainty about aggression is that a defensive (rather than an assertive) response will aggravate the situation. However, it takes considerable maturity on the part of the parent to stay separate, firm and calm in response to a son's or daughter's aggression. Because parents perceive their child's response as a criticism or a rejection of them, they feel hurt, and the tendency is to lash back. It helps enormously when parents can stay separate from their child's aggression and read the difficult behaviour as being one hundred per cent about the perpetrator and not saying an iota about the receiver. The reason for each child's (or parent's) aggression is unique, but it is safe to say that some perceived hurt, rejection, misunderstanding or threat preceded the aggression. When the dust has settled and the parent has followed the procedures outlined above, the mature response is to provide as much safety and love as possible and to enquire what has hurt or threatened your son or daughter.

THE REALITY OF FAMILY LIFE

The most common illusion is that 'we all come from happy families'. This is a clever creation, because it considerably lessens the chances that the shortcomings that exist in each family will be voiced. Obviously, the extent of light and darkness is on a continuum from low to very high and varies from one family to another. Breaking the silence on the reality that family life is a mixed bag of joyful and neglectful experiences is not easy. The dangers are aggressive or silent treatment reactions from other family members, accusations of betrayal, outright rejection, violence, breaking off contact, labelling you as 'mad', 'bad' or 'sad', and a concerted effort of others in the family to maintain the illusion. There is no doubt that everyone wants to belong to a family, to a partner, to a group or to the workplace. However, individuals are frequently disappointed, demeaned, hurt, disillusioned and traumatised because of an over-belonging or an under-belonging or total neglect.

The over-belonging family is where little separateness is allowed and the parent(s) lives his or her life through the children. The controlling message is 'I am there for you and you must always need me'. It is very difficult to escape the stranglehold of over-caring, because it might come across that you are being ungrateful. The refrain 'after all I've done for you' may haunt your bid for freedom and your expression of your individuality, difference and creativity. It may appear safer to develop the illusion that 'my parent is so wonderfully giving of herself and I'm so grateful to have her as a parent'. However, not breaking the silence on a parent's neglect of her own personal development and unhealthy enmeshment with her children is where real betrayal lies, because both parent and children will remain imprisoned in this family's conditional world. Both the parent and children deserve the opportunity to come fully into their sacred presence, to be separate from each other, to realise their own individuality, difference and giftedness and to respond to the deepest longing of both child and adult – the need for unconditional love.

The under-belonging family has the parent architect who subconsciously projects that the children and partner are there for him (or her) and that therefore they must live life according to his ways, values, wishes and expectations. This is the dominant parent who overpowers through a torrent of 'shoulds', 'should nots', 'have to's', 'ought to's', and children dare not assert differently. The relationship is conditional and demands conformity to the dominant will of the parent. The consequences are a darkening of the unique presence of each child, a disrespect for individuality or difference and the right to discover one's own unique way of experiencing life. Any attempt to assert independence can be rubbished. Children who acquiesce hide their true self, whilst those who rebel attempt to counter-control, but do not achieve separateness and independence. The illusion that 'my parent has my best interests at heart' needs to be broken, as much for the oppressed children as for the parent who behaves narcissistically. It is an act of love to confront this untenable situation and an act of neglect to stay silent.

In a family where total neglect exists, neither the child's person nor the child's behaviour merits any love or recognition. This is the darkest place to be, and children in these situations learn to hide every aspect of their sacred selves.

The defensive image they present to the world may be of apathy, depression, alcohol or drug addiction, violence, delinquency and total irresponsibility. They have had no models for loving self and others, and they remain invisible to self and others until some patient hand is extended to help them come into their special presence. Silence about such gross neglect weighed heavily on our culture up to and during the 1980s, but, thankfully, the voices of the neglected are being heard and listened to more and more.

A child's environment should always be worthy of his or her unique person and dignity. Scott Peck, author of *The Road Less Travelled*, advises that 'children need to be given over to life and not to parents'. There is wisdom in this, but parents themselves require a strong possession of their own interiority before they have the solid ground from which to love and support their children's expression of their unique presence. When parents bring the emotional baggage of not belonging to themselves into their relationships with each other and their children, they are not ready for the provision of unconditional love and the recognition of their children's uniqueness and drive to express their individuality and explore their vast giftedness and potential. Parents cannot give children what they have not got themselves. Indeed, parents can only bring their children to the same level of realisation of self and others that they have reached themselves. For that reason, parents, who are the architects of the family culture, have a duty to examine their own internal architecture and to ensure that its foundations are solid and its building expansive, creative and inspiring. Social agencies have the responsibility to create the opportunities for training for parenting, and parents have the responsibility to learn to parent themselves before they take on or continue the parenting of children.

CHILDREN IN DISTRESS

It is not difficult for adults to identify the child who is troubled. What is difficult, particularly for the parents (and sometimes teachers), is to admit to the fact that the child may be undergoing a crisis. I have known of parents who, out of subconscious defensiveness, have rationalised that 'it's a passing phase' or 'it's due to his diet' or some other vague biological explanation. When parents are in a place of denial or rationalisation, it is they who need help first. Indeed, the very fact that the parents feel emotionally threatened by their child's troubled symptoms indicates that the possible cause of the child's distress lies within the family. Of course, not all troubled behaviour in children can be traced to family dynamics. Children can be under emotional, physical, social and sexual threat within the other social systems they frequent – school, community and sports clubs.

Signs of children's hidden conflicts can be usefully grouped under these headings:

☐ Physical signs
☐ Undercontrol signs
☐ Overcontrol signs

Examples of possible physical signs of distress are: nailbiting, bedwetting, soiling, headaches, abdominal pain, jumping at sudden noises, involuntary muscle spasms, obesity, skin problems.

Signs of undercontrol include those behaviours that may be very troublesome and annoying to others but are, none-heless, clear signs of emotional distress. Children displaying these signs are acting out their inner turmoil in a sub-conscious attempt to get their unmet needs recognised and attended to. Typical undercontrol signs of distress are rebellious behaviours, verbal aggressiveness, destructiveness of property, hyperactivity and bullying. Psychologically, these difficult behaviours are saying something right about the child's hidden emotional distress, but socially the behaviours can make it difficult for parents and others. The danger is that parents can respond defensively to these manifestations, thereby adding fuel to the fire with the resultant escalation of the child's undercontrol behaviours. The 'out-of-control' punishing response by parents serves only to convince the child of his inadequacy and unlovability, and plunges him into further depths of insecurity. Because children's under-control behaviours can be so upsetting to other family members, some constructive action is of course needed to try to reduce or eliminate them. However, such a course of action will have little chance of being effective if it is not coupled with attempts to understand what is emotionally troubling the child.

Overcontrol signs of distress are more common in girls than in boys. Examples include shyness, passivity, perfectionism, timidity, over-pleasing, feelings easily hurt. These manifes-tations do not in any serious way disrupt the lives of others; quiet, shy children do not interfere with parents in carrying out their domestic and other responsibilities. It is for this reason that children showing undercontrol signs of distress are more often sent to clinical psychologists or counsellors for help. Unfortunately, the children who are perfectionistic, timid and fearful are more at risk emotionally than those children who 'act out' their feelings of rejection and inade-quacy. It is as if those who shout loudest are most likely to be heard.

The hope is that children, whether they exhibit undercontrol or overcontrol signs of distress, will have their emotional conflicts detected and effectively responded to, and that more adaptive ways of expressing their fears, worries and insecurities will be modelled and taught to them.

The first step is to *listen*. Listening is an act of worship, and when parents show genuinely that they want to actively listen, children may open up and reveal their inner worries. The second step is to understand. The word 'understand', when it is broken down to under-stand, sets the course of action required. The child's stand may be aggression (undercontrol) or timidity (overcontrol), and what the parent needs to do is get under or go beneath the behavioural signs and discover what is causing the child's distress.

Patience is essential because it provides the safety for children to reveal why they are behaving in troubled ways. Any attempt on the part of parents to force their way into the hidden world of a child will only result in the child heightening and expanding his protectors.

The third requirement is *compassion*. Compassion provides the unconditional love and intuitive wisdom that *knows* that children are not deliberately trying to make their parents' lives difficult but are attempting to bring to the fore what they dare not reveal.

I can guarantee parents that when they actively listen, understand, be patient and show compassion, their children will open up and will in turn show the same wise responses to them.

ADOLESCENTS IN HIDING

Self-esteem is the 'in-thing'. Adults are expected not only to know about self-esteem, but are also expected to possess a strong sense of themselves if they are to be effective as parents or workers or teachers or managers or employers. It is now well established that the way in which adults and children view themselves influences everything they do, think, say and feel.

A clear distinction needs to be made between self-worth and self-esteem. Self-worth is your real and authentic self. The self-worth of infants is very evident; they are spontaneous, affectionate, able to receive love, highly intelligent, confident, they love learning, they are naturally curious, they are amazing at making their needs known and they are sure of their unique presence. Furthermore, success and failure have no effect on them; they trip, they fall, they succeed, but no matter what the outcome of their actions, they progress onto the next challenge. Many children, adolescents and adults have gone a long, long distance from that original place of sureness. The measure of your vulnerability is the distance from your real self.

Self-esteem is a screen self, a shadow self, a crust that children form around their real selves. This crust protects the unique pearl of their self-worth and it reduces further threats to their expression of their true presence. It is not that parents, teachers, relatives and other significant adults in children's lives want deliberately to push children into hiding their real selves, but they themselves lie in hiding and they operate out from their shadow selves. Your shadow self does not reflect the shape of your uniqueness, individuality and sacredness. In order to be accepted, children ingeniously conform to the shadow behaviours and expectations of parents and others. Such conformity brings the comfort of feeling less threatened and attaining some kind of acceptance. However, the acceptance is conditional on certain behaviours and never truly reaches the hearts of children. Insecurity will dog their steps until such time that opportunities arise for them to free themselves of the prison of living in shadow-lands. Sometimes the opportunities for change arise when their parents or other important adults in their lives come into their own enlightened presence.

Some children and young people rebel against the shadow behaviours of others, but this is shadow begetting shadow, and a deeper darkness invades relationships. The aim is to counter-control, but the very behaviours that are threatening to those who rebel are the very ones used to reduce hurt. These young people are not free but are imprisoned by the battle to offset further blows to their self-worth. 'An eye for and eye and a tooth for a tooth' never brought peace within or between the combatants. Examples of shadow behaviours of adults that throw young people into hiding are:

□ irritability
□ dismissiveness
□ aggression
□ passivity
□ unrealistic expectations
□ apathy
□ over-protection
□ lack of affection
□ violence
□ dominance
□ rigidity

- perfectionism
- fear of failure
- addiction to work
- addiction to success
- anxiety
- depression

The frequency, intensity and endurance (years, months, weeks) of these behaviours are telling factors in establishing how shadowed a person is.

Parents who engage in and experience any of the above-listed behaviours deserve compassion, not judgment. Judging them will only propel them into stronger defensive behaviours, whereas compassion may provide the first stepping stone towards redeeming their true selves.

Adolescents can have either transient or more enduring shadow responses. The transient ones have largely to do with the new challenges that adolescence brings – gaining acceptance by peer group, sexual development, experience of sexual attraction, increased academic competitiveness, greater educational responsibilities and major school examinations that have a determining influence on their future educational and career prospects. The transient defensive reactions may be:

- worrying about having a pleasing personality
- examination anxiety
- concern about physical appearance
- wanting to be liked
- 'hard man' behaviour
- shyness
- rebelliousness
- anxiety about not having enough money
- sexual insecurity

The more alarming shadow behaviours that a high percentage of adolescents show are:

- perfectionism
- intense worry about examinations
- wanting to drop out of school
- having no friends
- feeling unattractive
- hating self
- pessimism and fatalism
- never feeling good enough
- avoidance of contact with peers
- intense shyness
- strong feeling that nobody likes them
- terror of failure
- isolation
- depression
- high anxiety
- suicidal feelings and thoughts
- aggression
- refusal to listen or accept help

With regard to the transient shadow responses, parents can rest assured that further life experience will resolve these uncertainties for their adolescent offspring. However, the more enduring and intense defensive behaviours are a serious cause for concern. Sadly, when parents themselves act out from a dark interiority, sometimes they are not in a place to see that not only their children but they themselves need help to resolve the deep insecurities that darken the family. Denials, blaming of others and covering up the problems are all too common responses, and sometimes it takes a tragedy before help is sought.

TEENAGE REBELLION

The most vulnerable time of a person's development is the first seven years of life. It is during this time that emotional, social, intellectual, physical and spiritual processes are formulated and the basic rules of life are laid down. Without a sound spiritual link, many erroneous belief systems become the ground on which perception of self, others and the world is based. One of the principal reasons why this occurs is that during these formative years, children are totally dependent on their parents or guardians for love, food, warmth, clothing and shelter.

Therefore, if a child is told that she will not receive food unless she is good, then she will be good. If a child is told to be brave and not to cry and then he will be loved, then he will not cry. If a child is told that if she achieves highly in school she will be cherished, then she will overwork to achieve academically. Such belief systems will continue to influence the actions and self-worth of the child into later years.

Thankfully, there comes a time when there is less dependence, a time when it is necessary to challenge the wisdom of these beliefs and to see whether they still hold true in the present environment and are in harmony with the individual's own inner truth.

If there is disharmony, then conflict necessarily develops, which in the adolescent years is described by besieged adults as the 'rebellious stage'. This is when young people are attempting to maturely determine what is true for them as individuals and what belongs to their parents and society.

They may appear to go overboard with wild hair-styles, 'way-out' clothing, bizarre beliefs, outrageous friends and unrecognisable music. This is their attempt to present the opposite role of existence to that experienced by their parents. However, experimenting with new ways can often appear quite daunting, as the old ways feel familiar and comfortable. There is often a fear of 'how will my parents and others react?' The admonishments 'I told you so' or 'don't say I didn't try to warn you' are not helpful when young people are attempting to set out alone.

When the old belief systems involve repeated messages that darken or dull a young person's presence, it can be very difficult for him to start to develop some degree of self-identity and realise his self-worth. The only role left to such an individual is often that of believing that all that happens is his fault and that he will never succeed in anything that he attempts. As he begins to develop a small degree of self-worth, he may even feel guilty for denying that which he has believed for so long. He can become both the victim and the victimiser and growth can become static. In truth, the young person is the only one who holds the key to freeing himself from his prison – many can offer support, love and encouragement, but the teenager needs to unlock the door to allow true friends to enter. Everything takes time, and one of the clever ways of sabotaging any forward movement is to set the goals too high and thereby fulfill the subconscious belief that nothing is possible. Whatever the reason, change is always difficult and threatening, particularly if the home, school, church and community are not supportive of questioning old beliefs.

Between the ages of twelve and twenty, many young people tentatively formulate their own belief systems and apply them in their early adult years. In their late twenties they reintroduce the more mature aspects of their parents' standards and combine them with their own beliefs. However, there are many individuals who pass quietly through the teenage rebellion, only to see it emerge in their middle-age. I can also think of a goodly number of people in their fifties and sixties whose actions are still ruled by the belief systems of their parents.

Rules and belief systems need to be assessed, not just in adolescence, but throughout the whole of our lives, to check that they are still in harmony with intuitive wisdom. Such wisdom comes through the development of intuition and will reflect that which is good not only for the individual but also for humanity as a whole.

WOMEN HIT TOO!

The NSPCC defines violence as being hit with a hand, an implement or a fist, kicked hard, shaken, thrown or knocked down, beaten up, choked, burnt or threatened with a knife or a gun. Statistics bear out that approximately 25 per cent of families experience physical violence. There is a myth that nearly 100 per cent of such violence in the home is perpetrated by men. However, a recent study of children who had been victims of violence found that 49 per cent said their mother was the aggressor and 40 per cent stated their father was the aggressor.

I do not find these statistics surprising, because women still do 90 per cent of the parenting, and lone parents are predominantly female. Parenting is such a self-sacrificing and highly demanding profession, without any training, that it should not come as a shock that women can resort to physical control of their children. Indeed, in breaking the silence on the fact that some women can physically violate their children, there is no intention to judge or in any way demean women. On the contrary, the aim is to understand, help and support these parents to deal more constructively with the strains and countless demands of parenting.

It does not mean that women who perpetrate violence do not love their children; rather the recourse to physical punishment arises from not knowing more respectful and effective ways of dealing with children who can test one's patience to its limit. However, to say that 'the child drove me to it' is not going to resolve the use of violence. This 'passing the buck' of responsibility for a parent's violent actions onto the child means there is no ownership of the threatening actions and their sad consequences. Progress can only occur when the mother accepts the fact of her violence and that she is fully responsible *to* it. Mothers (or fathers) are not responsible *for* their violence, as this would imply deliberate and cold use of violence to control children. My own experience is that violent actions arise from a deep source of insecurity, hurt, fear and vulnerability and are subconsciously intended to reduce threats to the besieged parent. Parents do not intentionally want to violate the sacredness of a child's body, but they do want to appear in control so that they will not be criticised as being 'bad' parents.

Understanding and finding the reasons for the use of physical punishment is vital to its resolution. It is neither possible nor wise to generalise on the reasons for violence. Each person who engages in such demeaning behaviour needs to reflect on what causes them to act in this way. It may be hating self, perfectionism, having to be in control, living your life through children, feeling rejected, rigidity, dependence, grief, stress, financial problems, threat to family image, repeating violent pattern from home of origin. The possible causes can be as many as the people who perpetrate violence. Over the years I have learned that each person who comes for help needs a different type of helping response. I have also observed that the actions outside self are mirrors of the nature of the relationships you have inside yourself. The only enduring change is that which comes from within, because that will wholly determine your actions. Possibilities are that you need to:

- Love and accept self
- Embrace failure
- Separate out from family of origin

- □ Free self from having to prove yourself to gain recognition
- □ Value your own beliefs, opinions and needs
- □ Give yourself permission to ask for what you want
- □ Seek support
- □ Create solid boundaries that do not tolerate any lessening of you by children or other adults

Being human is recognising that any of us, whether female or male, when physically or emotionally or socially or sexually threatened, can resort to the most devastating of physical and verbal weaponry. But being human is also to recognise that we have immense wisdom to understand and resolve actions that put ourselves and others at risk. Reaching out for help and support is often a good 'starting point'.

Yardsticks for determining whether professional help may be required are the frequency, intensity and endurance of the violent episodes. We all lose control now and again, but once we apologise and are genuinely determined to learn from the loss of control, then its effects will be minimal. However, when the loss of control occurs daily or several times weekly, when it is severe and harsh and lasts beyond minutes and is recurring over months or years, then seeking help from a psychologist or counsellor is expedient.

MOTHERS UNDER FIRE AGAIN

Young children who spend most of their time being cared for by someone other than their mother are more likely to show behavioural problems, according to a new US survey. The study suggests that small children who spend more than thirty hours a week in daycare or in the care of a nanny or family relation – anyone other than the mother – were three times more likely to be aggressive, defiant, demanding and disobedient when they went to nursery school or kindergarten. The study was conducted over a ten year period, and followed more than 1,100 children in ten cities in a wide range of care settings – in play centres, in daycare groups, cared for by nannies or by relatives, in preschool and in kindergarten. The researchers claim that the findings were not related to the type or quality of the childcare given or the gender of the child. They also say that the results hold true regardless of the family's socio-economic status. The conclusions were based on interviews and observational ratings by the children's mothers, as well as by those caring for them and nursery school teachers.

There is no doubt that the study has unearthed an issue that demands attention, but whether or not that issue is related to children being placed into a caring situation within three to four months of birth rather than being with their mothers is questionable. Uni-variable research is fraught with all sorts of problems, the most significant being the part played by factors not measured by the study. What is noticeably lacking in the study is any reference to the father. How long is the prejudice going to remain that fathers cannot be the primary carers of children? I would be curious to know whether or not, if the father was the stay-at-home parent, would the children become three times more aggressive? Neither did the study indicate how many of the children were members of a two-parent or lone parent or reconstituted family! I imagine the study is going to trigger a strong defensive reaction from working mothers, and rightly so.

Though the study claims that the results were not related to the type or quality of childcare received, I doubt that any effort was made to observe the emotional quality of the care that the children received. After all, parenting is the most difficult profession of all, requiring commitment, unparalleled self-sacrifice and the skills to cope with the physical, emotional, social, behavioural, intellectual, educational, creative, sexual, recreational and spiritual development of children. Quite a tall order for any parent, particularly when they also need to keep their own personal development on a par with what they would like for their children. The reality is that parents (and, indeed, childminders and care agencies) can only bring children to the same level of development that they have reached themselves. How many parents and others who care for children possess those kinds of resources? Other factors that the study may have missed are:

- ☐ Employed parents are tired and stressed
- ☐ Marital conflict
- ☐ Self-esteem level of parent
- ☐ Self-esteem level of children studied
- ☐ Modelling of aggressive behaviours by adults with whom children interact
- ☐ Level of stimulation within the home
- ☐ Exposure to video, TV and Internet violence

As regards the last issue on the list, we know that children are affected by the violence they see via the TV, VCR or the Internet, but have we taken it seriously when they are in their daily lives actually (other than virtually) exposed to violence, intimidation and cruelty?

In the last decade, particularly due to the rise of violence among children in Middle America, there is much more commitment to discovering the root causes of these seemingly unattributable outbreaks of child violence. It is good and necessary that researchers continue to investigate the causes of violent and aggressive behaviour in children and adults. However, human behaviour is individual, social, complex and multi-faceted, and a cautious and holistic approach is needed before causes can be truly inferred.

BOYS WILL BE GIRLS!

The seven massacres of children and adults by children in America between 1997 and 1999 have led to a backlash against 'boys being boys' and a move towards making 'boys more like girls'. This is a misguided notion because violence perpetrated by male adults and children is not a gender but a socialisation and discipline issue. Neither does the problem lie in boys being over-masculinised, although boys being under-feminised is definitely a contributory factor. It is amazing the number of professionals who confuse being male with masculinity and being female with femininity. Gender is about being male or female and it is essential that boys be male and girls be female. The qualities of masculinity and femininity have to do with the two major groups of human characteristics that are essential for maturity in *both* males and females. Much of boys' tendencies to violence arise from a lack of feminine human characteristics rather than from a surfeit of masculine ones. It is unlikely that boys or men who can nurture, care and feel for others would be physically or mentally cruel. Similarly, girls who are much more inclined towards passivity are not over-feminised but under-masculinised. It is also unlikely that females who are equipped with the masculine human characteristic of assertiveness would turn a blind eye to any neglect of self or of another. The more that people fault masculinity in itself for violence by male children, the deeper one shadows the real causes – an imbalance of human characteristics not only in males but also in females, and a weakening of moral education and discipline.

Effective socialisation of both male and female children must focus on the development of the full expansiveness of human behaviour, which means both masculine and feminine characteristics. The masculine behaviours in males have accounted for much of what is progressive in the world:

- □ logical thinking
- □ physical strength
- □ drive
- □ assertiveness
- □ dynamism
- □ energy
- □ initiative
- □ outward movement

Equally, the feminine attributes in females account for much of what is right in the world:

- □ nurturance
- □ emotional expressivity
- □ passivity
- □ intuition
- □ inward movement
- □ commitment

What accounts for much of what is wrong in the world is either males not having been encouraged to develop the human characteristics of emotional sensitivity, intuition and nurturance, or females having been blocked from taking on the masculine behaviours of drive, logical thinking and outward movement. There is no doubt that in the last two decades women have considerably expanded their behavioural repertoire to include the masculine characteristics of assertiveness, initiative and outward movement. Regrettably, males have largely remained floundering in the quagmire of the imbalance of high masculinity and low femininity. Certainly, the reduction of violence among males will be helped by correcting this imbalance in their socialisation; also the confusion of male with masculinity and female with femininity must also be extinguished.

It is of vital importance that school, work, community, national and home cultures are infused with a moral content and climate that will ensure mutual respect for each member, and that any physical, emotional and social violations are unthinkable and always unacceptable. Furthermore, when either minor or major violations occur in relation to an individual's rights to physical, sexual, emotional, intellectual and spiritual safety, appropriate disciplining responses must follow. Unfortunately, all the signs indicate that the character development of many children is being neglected, that violations of people's rights are not being disciplined and that a *laissez faire* attitude to values development abounds.

Boys do not need to be rescued from masculinity and they do not need to be made to play with dolls, but they do need opportunities and permission to broaden their ways of coping with the world. Similarly, girls do not need to be rescued from femininity, but they do need to continue to become expansive in their adoption of the full range of human characteristics. All young people deserve a social environment that is respectful of all, that is fair, just, inclusive, that promotes equality within genders and between genders, and that does not tolerate violations of people's rights. Neglect of these issues of character development, healthy and broad socialisation, moral education and discipline puts both children and adults at risk.

PREMATURE LEAVE-TAKING

A sizeable number of young people who leave home to pursue third-level education or career development do not fare well in their home leave-taking and can experience considerable emotional and social trauma in their new situations. Their homesickness means that they are not in a place to apply themselves to their studies, and this is probably one of the main reasons for the high failure and drop-out rate in the first year of third-level education. Somehow these young fledglings were not ready for their freedom flight and they are suffering from premature leave-taking. A good percentage return home, but very often the causes of their return are not looked at and their immaturity goes unchallenged.

It is essential that parents ensure that their young adult offspring are ready for the challenges that face them in the outside world. When readiness is not apparent, then intervention will be required to bring them to that place of confidence. Young people who experience premature leave-taking are identifiable by a range of behaviours:

- frequently feeling homesick
- feeling confused away from home
- lacking concentration
- frequently crying
- telephoning home on a daily basis
- going home as often as possible
- complaining of feeling unhappy and not coping
- frequently asking for help and reassurance
- refusing to make contact with peers

- ☐ being withdrawn, moody and easily upset
- ☐ being indecisive

The frequency, intensity and duration of these signs of premature leave-taking are important considerations in determining what level of help and support will be needed. Frequency has to do with how often any of the signs occur – is it once or twice a week, every day, several times a day? Intensity is a measure of the emotional threat exhibited when the young person manifests his or her insecurity. Would you rate it as mildly, moderately or seriously distressing to the unhappy person? Duration has to do with how long these behaviours have persisted, and, on a particular occasion, how long the symptoms last – is it a minute, several minutes, an hour, a day?

Certainly, it is the case that many young people experience homesickness in the early weeks of leaving home, but as they adjust to their new circumstances they settle into the challenge of separating out from home. However, there are others who persistently show the signs of premature leave-taking, and there is no indication of any improvement in their coping.

Very often, when parents look honestly at their children's difficulties in adjusting to being away from home, they can see that their insecurities preceded their leaving home and that the challenges necessary to become independent were neither set nor pursued.

There are a host of reasons why some young people fare poorly on their first flight from the nest:

- ☐ over-protective parenting
- ☐ over-involved relationships with one or both parents
- ☐ socially isolated upbringing

- few opportunities to socialise in early years
- parents very housebound
- symbiotic family that excluded most social contact with outside world
- young person feeling responsible for parents left at home
- young person feeling guilty about leaving parents
- lack of confidence
- poor sense of self

It is essential for parents to be loving and empathic towards their troubled son or daughter. Every opportunity needs to be taken to enhance self-worth. Indeed, parents may need to look at their own level of coping and admit to their own lack of confidence and their responsibility to do something about it. An expression of regret for not being in a place to adequately prepare their son or daughter for the adventure of leaving home always helps.

Parents are advised not to make the mistake of telling the young adults what their problem is; it is best that they are allowed to define their own problems, what they feel has brought them to this difficult stage and what kind of help do they now require to resolve their plight? No criticism, cajoling, comparisons, pushing or ridiculing must occur, as these reactions will only further undermine the young person's self-worth and confidence. Furthermore, do not give advice unless requested. Do accept where they are at and respond to their needs. Sometimes they may need to come home and postpone college. Active listening is essential and so is patience.

The priority must be the young person's emotional and social well-being and not academic or career progress. When the first two attributes are not present, it is unlikely that the latter will emerge. In any case, it is more expedient for the young person to explore his or her inner world and find ways to come into the fullness of his or her worth, value, uniqueness, individuality and limitless potential. Parents have a responsibility to provide the belated opportunities for such developments. Sometimes professional support and guidance may be needed.

THE DECLINE OF THE FAMILY

There is a startling rise in lone-parent families and the absence of paternal involvement. Depending on geographical and social location, anything between 30 to 40 per cent of babies are being born to the female single parent. For many women, this is a matter of deliberate choice. Of course, men are needed to get these women pregnant in the first place and to provide financial support for the child, but usually this is on an informal basis afterwards. It would appear that the role of men as husband and father is being steadily eroded.

In the traditional two-parent family, the role of the father tended to be largely limited to being the breadwinner. However, there had been signs in the last decade that men were showing their feminine side and becoming more involved in the nurturance of their children. Also equalisation between the sexes in terms of career development, domesticity, finance and social independence was emerging.

I am not suggesting that individuals should stay in unhappy marriages or families. Indeed, all the evidence is that children fare far better in a happy one-parent family than in a conflictual two-parent family. However, there is over-whelming evidence that the stable two-parent family results in children faring better in school and in later life. No other family arrangement comes close.

There is another serious consideration to not evaluating the modern trend where long-term commitment is no longer so highly valued and marriage not seen as a desirable option.

The issue is the emotional, social and physical well-being of both men and women. Single men, next to married career women, show the highest risk of cancer and early death. The emotional and social benefits of marriage and family have not been appreciated and broadcasted. Furthermore, the responsibility of fathering, in its broadest sense, helps to mature men. Sociologists in America have shown that without the responsibility of fatherhood, men often become irresponsible, drift from job to job and may even descend into criminal activities. It is also known that the lone female parent, whether through choice or the enforced circumstances of separation, divorce or death of spouse, is far more stressed compared to the mother in a two-parent stable family.

I do not believe that the way forward, as some authors have suggested, is to financially sanction lone parenting and reward dual parenting. But I do believe that it would be very unwise to dismiss the rapid demise of the two-parent family. Fatherless families should be the exception, not the norm. Lone-parent families need not be an inevitable development, and there is no reason why the present trend cannot be reversed. However, it is going to take considerable political and social will to reverse what has happened. In the preoccupation with the present economic boom, it does not seem that the Irish government or even opposing political parties are willing to 'bite the bullet' on the issue. The groundswell for change may need to come from the churches, voluntary bodies and progressive groups, who are concerned to promote what is best for the total well-being of both adults and children.

One of the vital tasks that is required immediately is sound research on the causes, maintenance factors and the experience of lone parenting. It may well be that women who choose this lifestyle are having emotional, social and identity needs met that were not being recognised elsewhere. Other possibilities are disillusionment with marriage or with men who have abandoned them, and a desire for financial independence. Unless the causes are found we are unlikely to stem the tide.

Media promotion of the emotional, social and physical advantage of the stable two-parent family and long-term commitment between adults would certainly help to push the boat out on reversing the trend. Also, education for relationships, both couple and familial, has always been lacking, and this development would offer a strong boon to stopping the decline of the two-parent family.

LETTING GO IS HARD TO DO

There are a sizeable number of men and women who remain tied to their mother's apron strings or to their father's control. These entrapped adult children have never left home; even within the confines of the home, some of these adults have not found their own physical space — either they occupy the same rooms as their parents or their own rooms are invaded frequently by their parents.

Outside the home they have neither strong emotional nor social connections. They are inextricably emotionally bound up with their parents and are subconsciously fearful of establishing any emotional commitments outside the home. Their relationship with their parents is still a child-parent one and there is no support or encouragement from parents or from other members of the family who have flown the nest, to free themselves of their emotional prison.

There are many reasons why such unhealthy relationships develop between parents and adult children:

- a parent's own emotional baggage
- parenting that was possessive or dominating
- the transfer of unmet emotional needs to a son or daughter from a spouse who proved disappointing
- the belief that children are there for parents
- realistic fears of loneliness

All of these reasons show a failure in effective parenting, and also a failure on the part of the parents to address their own vulnerabilities and dependencies and seek help to resolve them. Denial is a strong characteristic of parents who hold onto their children; they neither see the plight of their entrapped son or daughter nor their own unhappy enmeshment and poor self-reliance. This is a subconscious defense and works powerfully to maintain the status quo and avoid having to face difficult challenges.

There is no intention here to blame parents: they are victims of their childhoods and of the emotional baggage they carried into their marriage and newly formed family. Nonetheless, there is a responsibility on all adults to ensure that they do not pass on their problems to others, particularly to children. After all, children are dependent on parents for love, warmth, nurturance, shelter, education and clothing, and they cannot afford to risk going against parents who block their emotional, social, sexual and spiritual progress. Conformity becomes a necessary survival strategy. The more intense and enduring the parents' blocks to children's freedom, the more difficult it is to cut the umbilical cord later on as a young or older adult. Nonetheless, adult children who continue to remain at home have a duty to love themselves, assert their own individuality, uniqueness and capability and their right to live their own lives.

There are a number of behaviours that are typical of adults who remain stuck at home:

- □ being childish and dependent
- □ being timid and fearful
- □ conforming to values, morals and wishes of parents
- □ lacking in confidence
- □ few or no contacts outside home
- □ no intimate relationship
- □ taking responsibility for parents' well-being
- □ avoiding challenges

Each one of the above behaviours poses a challenge to go in the opposite direction:

- become adult and independent
- realise your own power
- determine your own values, morals and wishes
- build up your confidence
- make contacts outside home
- form an intimate relationship
- allow parents to take responsibility for themselves
- take on challenges

However, it is not easy to achieve emancipation, and, because the risks are high, clever rationalisations are voiced:

- 'My parents need me.'
- 'My parents have done so much for me; it is my duty to do the same for them.'
- 'My parents wouldn't hear of my leaving.'
- 'I would feel so guilty about leaving.'

There is no doubt that the effort to tell parents that 'it is time I began to live my own life' means risking the consequences of rejection, hostility, silent treatment and even parents becoming sick. However, there is a hidden issue and that is the fear of these individuals themselves that they will not be able to cope on their own. This is not surprising, as they have not had the opportunities to stand on their own two feet, to hold their own no matter how difficult or trying things may be. What is sad is that the very dependence that led their parents to block their progress has now been repeated in them. A build-up of emotional and social skills, the creation of mature relationships and financial independence are going to be needed to prepare for their freedom flight. What helps enormously is support outside the home. In extreme cases professional support may be required.

Finally, it does help when these adult children realise that their parents managed without them the twenty to thirty years or more before they were born. Also, their emancipation is the opportunity to create a mature, ongoing adult to adult relationship with their parents. Letting go does not mean breaking off relationships.

PARENTS WHO REFLECT ARE MORE EFFECTIVE

'Know thyself' is an ancient dictum, but one that has time-less relevance to all of us, particularly to parents, teachers and other professional people who have the responsibility of the care and guidance of children. It is well established that the way a parent feels about self influences everything he or she does, particularly how the children will feel about them-selves. However, it must not be forgotten that all significant adults in children's lives have an influence, especially grand-parents, teachers, childminders, relatives and community leaders. All of these adults would do well to reflect on how they feel about self and on how they relate to children.

There are two ways to reflect on these two issues — one is to look at how you typically treat self and how you interact with children. The second is to compare your daily actions to what you ideally need to do to feel good about self and to be an effective parent.

When you detect signs that you are downing yourself and/or children, it is important to see that these behaviours that demean self and children are opportunities, wake-up calls, to the realisation of self and the mature care of children.

Self-esteem is revealed in all sorts of ways, but how you look after yourself in your everyday life is a major revelation of how you feel about yourself. Check the following list and see how you fare in this regard.

CHECKLIST INDICATING SELF-NEGLECT

- Rushing and racing
- Missing meals
- Eating on the run
- Dependent on drugs (for example, Tagamet, tranquillisers, sleeping tablets, anti-depressants)
- Working long hours
- Frequently late for appointments
- Trying to do several things at the one time
- Rarely saying 'no' to demands made of you
- Having no time for self
- Few or no social outings
- Having little or no leisure time
- Lacking physical exercise
- Suffering from sleeplessness
- Overtired
- Rarely or never asking for help
- Overeating
- Undereating
- Dependent on alcohol
- Aggressive towards others
- Passive in the face of unrealistic demands or neglectful behaviours
- Manipulative
- Lacking caution (for example, don't wear seat-belt, drive with drink taken, carelessly cross busy thoroughfares)
- Having little family time
- Having to do everything perfectly
- Not taking care of your own or others' belongings
- Living in the future or in the past
- Fretful
- Worrying all the time

If you engage in one or more of the above behaviours, you are showing clear signs of poor regard for self. Clearly, the frequency, intensity and endurance of these behaviours are a further measure of the extent of self-neglect. An important further question to ask is how and to what extent are these daily ways affecting how you interact with your children. The following checklist may help you to identify how, from your place of self-neglect, you routinely interact with children. It is not that parents deliberately darken the presence of children, but they subconsciously act out from the darkness of their own interiority.

CHECKLIST ON INEFFECTIVE PARENTING

- ☐ Shouting at children
- ☐ Ordering, dominating and controlling children
- ☐ Using sarcasm and cynicism as means of control
- ☐ Ridiculing, scolding, criticising
- ☐ Labelling children as 'bold', 'stubborn', 'stupid', 'lazy', 'no good'
- ☐ Threatening children that the parent will leave them
- ☐ Threatening to send children away
- ☐ Physically threatening children
- ☐ Being physically violent
- ☐ Assigning punishments out of proportion to misdemeanours
- ☐ Pushing, pulling and shoving children
- ☐ Comparing one child with another
- ☐ Having an obvious favourite in the family
- ☐ Not calling children by their first names
- ☐ Being too strict
- ☐ Expecting too much of children
- ☐ Showing no interest in children's welfare
- ☐ Letting children slide out of responsibility
- ☐ Not showing affection to children
- ☐ Punishing mistakes and failures
- ☐ Never apologising for mistakes
- ☐ Not saying 'please' and 'thank you' to children
- ☐ Being inconsistent and unpredictable in response to children's irresponsible behaviours
- ☐ Allowing the children to control the parent
- ☐ Withdrawing love from children
- ☐ Using hostile silences to attempt to control children

Whilst parents are not to be judged or blamed for the above behaviours, they do have a responsibility to those actions that lessen children's presence. These signs point to parents' own neglect of themselves and their need to come into an acceptance of self and, from that solid base, to move towards positive rearing of their children.

Changing how you feel about self can only come through an intense, enduring, loving, accepting and affirming relationship with self. Indeed, the very actions towards children that will raise their self-esteem are the same as those that parents need to show to themselves. 'Love your child as yourself' is in keeping with the Christian message of 'Love your neighbour as yourself'. What children need of parents and what parents need of themselves are:

- Unconditional love
- Acceptance
- Physical holding
- Nurturance
- Praise of effort
- Affirmation of uniqueness
- Listening
- Time
- Challenge
- Positive talk
- Kindness
- Support
- Humour
- Positive firmness
- Advice on request
- Compassion
- Belief in
- Emotional responsivity

- ☐ Emotional expression
- ☐ Encouragement
- ☐ Fairness
- ☐ Apology when wrong

Parents' relationship with self is an endless process that needs to be consistently worked on at all times. The presence of parent self-care guarantees care of children.

PART THREE
EDUCATION

- Loving before learning
- Individuality and learning
- Belief, expectations and love of learning
- Embrace effort, failure and success
- Starting school
- Not so perfect!
- ADD – reality or myth?
- Multiple intelligence: a step in the wrong direction!
- To study or not to study
- Making homework positive
- Psychological absence in education
- Positive self-talk and examinations
- Self-observation: the key to teaching
- The caring school

LOVING BEFORE LEARNING

The prime need of both children and adults is to love and be loved. It is vital that parents and teachers see that love is a two-sided coin — both aspects of love need to be emphasised in their interactions with children. However, when a parent sees herself as the 'carer', she will have no difficulty in showing love to her children, but she will have difficulty in receiving it. The consequence of this is that the child learns that it is only safe to receive love, but not to give it. Any attempt to give love may result in withdrawal or criticism on the part of the 'carer'. Sadly, too, when a parent is tied to one side of the coin of love, her giving is conditional on children needing her, and children cleverly learn to be helpless and needy rather than powerful and independent.

Similarly, when a parent is only good at receiving love, but not at showing it, the child learns to give but not look for love. The child also perceives that the parent who is the 'taker' must not be disobeyed or contradicted, and this makes the parent's receiving of the child's love conditional.

It is only when parents and teachers are comfortable in both the giving and receiving of love that unconditional love is possible.

In the *Guidelines for Parents* of primary school children produced by the National Council for Curriculum and Assessment, there is no emphasis on the love relationship that needs to exist in the home and classroom if children are to maintain their eagerness to learn. The essential foundation for children's learning is that loving must always come before learning, and that learning must neither jeopardise children's sense of self nor the relationship between parents and children. However, if parents themselves experienced a loss of loving around their learning, then there is a danger that they will repeat it with their children. There are few of us who do not lose control with children when they fail or are slow to respond. However, what is needed immediately is a healing of the blow to the child's self-worth and the disruption of the parent-child relationship. A good index of a mature family is where parents apologise when they lose control or get it wrong. It is important that subsequent actions reinforce the verbal apology; otherwise children will learn not to trust the words of adults. When a parent apologises, he or she might say, for example, 'I'm sorry I shouted at you; that was no way to correct that behaviour. I still need you to do what I asked but I apologise for the way I did it.' When parents and teachers are comfortable in admitting loss of control and mistakes, it makes it more likely that children will imitate such mature behaviour; the contrary is also true.

Every child needs to shout from the rooftops: I am not my behaviour! Children deserve to be loved for themselves, for their unique and sacred presence. To love children for what they do and not for their person effectively dooms them to a life of dependence, insecurity and a hiding of their real presence. The distinction between person and behaviour is not a benign one, because confusing a child's person with a child's actions closes the door to their expression of their wonder and to an expansive life.

Not only does the enmeshment affect the prime need to love and be loved, it also affects the innate drive to know and understand the world. In other words, when learning threatens the need for unconditional loving, children will find ingenious ways to offset the rejection that can occur when parents or teachers are teaching them. The most common strategy is to avoid those knowledge areas where criticism or humiliation may result and to be attracted to those knowledge areas where no such threats occur. Other children employ aggression, hostility and uncooperative responses when threatened, and still others attempt to offset rejection by pressuring themselves to be the best in those knowledge areas that please their parents and teachers.

The other essential area that is overlooked in the recommendations to parents as partners in education is to make sure not to label children because of certain behaviours. Many children are labelled 'dull', 'slow', 'weak', 'stupid', 'thick', 'awkward', 'difficult', 'bad', and so on. Labelling confuses behaviour with the person of the child. It is okay to correct or encourage a certain behaviour, but be sure your comments are specific to the behaviour. Do not throw the baby out with the bathwater. Certainly correct the behaviour – 'I will not accept you hitting your brother' – but to say 'you're a bad boy' is unlikely to gain a responsible response from a child. The child intuitively knows that your putting him down over an unacceptable behaviour is akin to the pot calling the kettle black and that, in effect, your behavioural response is even more demeaning of a person's presence than his pushing his brother.

Similarly, the *Guidelines for Parents* would have done well to advise parents to praise behaviour, particularly learning efforts, rather than the children themselves. When you tell a child 'you're brilliant for coming top of the class', the child will associate your love with his brilliant behaviour and as a result may become success-addicted or, alternatively, may develop a fear of success. Either way, insecurity will haunt his learning. Praise, encouragement and reward are for *behaviours*, particularly for efforts to learn and the attainments that accompany each learning effort. Affirmation is for *person*, and children always deserve respect and love and acceptance of their uniqueness, difference and individuality and an acknowledgement of their unique giftedness and vast potential.

INDIVIDUALITY AND LEARNING

In the weeks leading up to the return to school after the summer holidays, many parents turn their minds to their children's academic progress. Children, on the other hand, continue to focus on their holiday activities or summer jobs and are not eager to listen to their parents' concerns or expectations. This difference in perspective often promotes conflict between parents and children, and the unhealthy admonishment of 'I know what's best for you' frequently emerges.

On that latter point, it is good for parents to know that children are quite well aware of what is best for them and what threatens their progress in this world. Not knowing what children are frightened of, on the other hand, can lead to parents and teachers putting pressure on children in directions that are not productive.

The emotional and social worlds of children become enmeshed with their intellectual and educational life. A major difficulty in classrooms is not the physical but the psychological absence of students. Mere physical presence does not in any way ensure learning. When children are not attentive, the concern is not their lack of attention but the need to discover why they are not present to the adventure of learning.

The prime need of children, and also of adults, is to love and be loved. The second most powerful need is to learn. Parents and teachers tend to see learning as what is taught in the classroom, and they often do not appreciate children's major learning adventures in emotionality, creativity, physicality, sensitivity, sociability, music, arts, sports, mechanics, play and spirituality.

When a child is not thriving in the academic subjects, most parents react in ways that do not benefit the child's progress. They may show annoyance, aggression or over-anxiousness, all of which are guaranteed to exacerbate the situation. They may compare the child to a sibling or a cousin or a neighbour, but comparisons are acts of emotional rejection and will cause either withdrawal or temper outbursts. In a world of individuals it makes absolutely no sense to compare.

One thing that parents can be assured of is that their child has an innate urge to express his or her own uniqueness, individuality and difference. Indeed, within the family, each child will ingeniously find a way to express his or her individuality and it is not at all unusual to find that children go the opposite to each other in emotional, social, physical and creative expression. Typically, within a family of four, you may have the 'academic', the 'carer', the 'charmer' and the 'athlete'.

It is wise for both parents and teachers to identify the unique ways in which children express their innate differences and, most importantly, to affirm that wonderful process. This does not mean allowing children to slide out of responsibilities that subconsciously they do not see as part of their identity. But it does mean that approaching areas of poor attainment and low motivation is done with sensitivity to the child's unique expression of self. When children are affirmed for their unique self-expression and when support and encouragement are given in what are perceived by parents and teachers as the 'difficult areas', positive movement is likely to occur.

One of the assumptions that parents may make regarding their child's poor to average academic progress is that he or she is 'weak' intellectually and that there is no point in trying 'to make a silk purse out of a sow's ear'. This response undermines the confidence of the child who has limitless ability to learn any field of knowledge. Lack of ability is not the issue but lack of motivation. Sometimes this lack of motivation may arise from one child's determination not to compete with an older sibling who is always 'top of the class'. Other times it may be that the child is carrying deep emotional doubts about being loved and seen for self, and school learning is not a priority issue. Other possibilities are peer pressure 'not to be smart', or bullying, or teachers who employ cynicism or sarcasm, or hidden violations that the child is terrified of revealing.

Only the individual child knows the true reasons for his or her poor motivation and low attainment levels, and only he or she can open the door to let you in to that inner world. Children are unlikely to let you in if you come banging on their door, or are over-anxious, or show little belief in them or compare them to others.

Patience, love, support, understanding and belief in children are what is needed for them to feel safe enough to bring us into their inner worlds. Parents also need to keep in mind that their responsibility is to support their children in their unique life journey and to let go of the notion that children are there to fulfil their (the parent's) projections.

BELIEF, EXPECTATIONS AND LOVE OF LEARNING

The level of *belief* that parents have in their children is the determining factor in the emergence of self-confidence, while the level of *expectations* that parents have of their children is the determining factor in the emergence of competence. Complaints of 'He doesn't believe in me' or 'She doesn't trust me' mirror belief difficulties. Complaints of 'He expects too much' or 'She doesn't expect enough' show difficulties around expectations. A clear distinction needs to be made between belief and expectations. Belief in a person is the essential building block of confidence; it is an affiration of the capability of the person. Expectations need to be addressed to the development of competence and have to do with the encouragement and creation of knowledge and skills. It is not uncommon to come across people who have a high degree of competence but little confidence; the opposite is less common.

Expectations can be realistic, unrealistic, absent or low. Realistic expectations centre on a person's present level of knowledge and set the next learning challenge just a little beyond that level. For example, a child may be able to put shoes on her feet but may not yet have identified the right from the left. The next step would be to get her to notice that each shoe is different.

Unrealistic expectations are typically performance driven, with the emphasis on getting things right. There is a failure to appreciate that there is an achievement in every learning effort, and that what counts most of all is that an effort to learn has been made. Unrealistic expectations make learning extremely threatening because the possibility of getting it right may be remote.

In some homes and workplaces people's love of learning may be gradually extinguished by parents or managers who have no expectations and who give little or no recognition to efforts to learn. Furthermore, because the parents or managers do not have expectations for themselves, the children or workers involved wisely assess that it is not safe to rise above the prevailing poor level of functioning. What is more common is the situation where parents and employers have low expectations and do not realistically challenge the children or workers involved.

Whilst the nature of learning and work expectations is a powerful determinant of whether or not people will retain their natural drive to learn, an equally powerful influence is how parents or employers react when children or workers fall short of, rise above or meet expectations.

Certainly, realistic expectations go a long way to maintaining people's love of learning and working, but this can be undermined if critical reactions follow failure to measure up to these reasonable demands. These critical reactions can take two forms: enmeshment of the falling short with the child's or the worker's person, and direct criticism of the failure experience. The latter is certainly the lesser of the two evils but, nonetheless, it poses a threat to future learning efforts and may result in the person cleverly devising protective strategies to offset that threat. Typical strategies are avoidance (with no effort there can be no failure; and with no failure there can be no rejection), compensation (with great effort there can be no failure; and with no failure there can be no humiliation) and rebelliousness (by getting somebody else to take on the challenge there can be no failure and therefore no rejection). Rebelliousness may accompany either avoidance or compensation. Another ingenious protective response is to become hypersensitive to criticism, act fearful and show visible upset when it is present. The aim of this strategy is similar to rebelliousness – get those who are threatening to back off with their critical attitudes.

The enmeshment of failure with person can be devastating to a person's eagerness to learn. Examples of this kind of reaction are 'Are you stupid or what?', 'Don't you see what you are doing wrong?' (said with exasperation), 'You're not paying attention' (said angrily). It is important to note that the non-verbal messages that accompany the verbal critical message lend considerable weight to the impact of the punishing feedback. Victims conclude from this kind of feedback that 'I'm stupid', 'I'm unlovable', 'I'm slow'. These self-labels often follow them for the rest of their lives and determine their inability to thrive occupationally. Someone who experiences enmeshment of person with failure may take up one of the protective strategies of avoidance, compensation, rebelliousness or timidity. Because the threats posed are great, the strategies may be employed to extremes, so that avoidance becomes apathy, compensation becomes perfectionism, rebelliousness becomes huge aggression, and timidity becomes utter helplessness.

Unrealistic expectations pose an enormous threat to the pursuance of learning and work, but when they are accompanied by punishing responses to failure to attain these high levels, the threat is greatly increased. Generally speaking, where there are unrealistic learning or work expectations, there is also the tendency to confuse person with failure.

Criticism can be expressed harshly, or great hurt and disappointment can be visibly shown. Powerful protective reactions are needed in response to these blows.

Positive over-reaction when individuals meet either realistic or unrealistic expectations is also a block to the emergence of confidence, but is often not seen as such. Examples are 'You're an amazing worker', 'You're a cut above the rest', 'You're great', 'We're so proud of you'. The difficulty with these responses is that those at the receiving end of such accolades become dependent on their accomplishments in order to be deemed worthy. They also know that falling short would result in emotional rejection ('You've let us down', 'You're not a company man', 'You're a disappointment').

Much can be done by parents and teachers to maintain the natural drive to learn and work that is evident in infants. Certainly, not confusing a child with his actions helps enormously. What also helps is the more subtle work of setting realistic expectations, showing belief in the limitless capacity of a child, embracing failure and success as equal stepping stones to further learning and viewing learning and work as an adventure, not a trial or a test. These recommendations to parents and teachers can be just as powerfully applied in the workplace.

EMBRACE EFFORT, FAILURE AND SUCCESS

There appears to be some confusion regarding the notion that learning, work, sports, creativity and productivity are best served by focusing on and valuing the effort involved in these pursuits. While there is no suggestion that the levels of achievements attained should not be celebrated, excellence is much more likely to emerge when people's attention is on the effort and process of learning rather than on the end result. In any case excellence can never be achieved without considerable effort; indeed, when excellence is not attained the problem generally will be in the level of effort shown. People who tend to focus on the end result will divide their energies between the process and the end result, and this means that their minds are operating both in the present and in the future. As a consequence, performance anxiety is the most common kind of fear and can be chronic and even crippling for some individuals. Failure and success are integral to learning; for the mature individual, both provide ongoing challenges. However, some people live for success and have a consequent dread of failure, and such fixations limit rather than enhance their creativity and productivity. Bill Gates put it well when he said: 'Success is the greatest impediment to progress.' It is unfortunate that success and failure are used as motivating forces: the result is either to diminish a love of learning or to create perfectionism or addiction to success. People who attempt to prove themselves through achievements, whether academic or nonacademic, are driven by fear, whereas those who love learning and work are driven by excitement and challenge.

The other issue regarding effort versus results is that, whilst a particular virtuoso performance deserves to be lauded, it is wise to keep the success separate from how you view the person who achieved it. What is often not appreciated is that children or adults who are labelled 'brilliant', 'genius', 'successful', 'wonderful', following high achievement in a particular knowledge or skill area often develop major performance anxiety, perfectionism and addiction to success. This phenomenon is due to these people's accurate assessment that 'my worthiness and value in this world is dependent on my performance, not on the uniqueness and sacredness of my person'. Sadly, only 3 per cent of so-called 'gifted' children make any important social contribution as adults. Their over-attention to the behaviour that gained them recognition not only bred massive insecurity, but also narrowed their fields of endeavour down to the 'success' area(s). Emotional, social, physical, sexual and spiritual illiteracy often result from addiction to success. Conversely, many children and adults who are labelled 'a fool', 'stupid', 'not too bright', 'average', have to hide their potential for fear of further ridicule. These individuals may demonstrate a weak knowledge of a particular subject and, certainly, that requires addressing, but in a way that does not put the person down but sets the next learning task.

Emphasis on performance also creates an unhealthy competitiveness, and results in comparisons between individuals who do poorly and those who achieve highly. Disillusionment and withdrawal are often the consequences for those who have been unfavourably criticised, while continued pressure to achieve is felt by those who demonstrate high performance.

The best form of competition is self-competition, where each individual is encouraged and supported to challenge themselves from their present level of attainment and not be looking over their shoulder at what others are doing. So many people, young and old, do not take on new challenges for fear of not being good enough and being compared to others. The wisdom of their avoidance is often missed by a society that is success- and competition-driven.

Certainly it is desirable to use superlatives to describe a laudable performance — 'brilliant', 'excellent', 'mind-boggling', 'superb', 'beyond expectation' – but individuals are not their behaviour. What is more worrying is that those who are labelled 'brilliant', etc., put themselves and others under considerable pressure and strain, and they are very prone to burnout. There is also the sad statistic that a high percentage of men die quite soon after retirement. These men have lost sight of the uniqueness of self and believe that their worth lies in their behaviour.

While society benefits greatly from the efforts and attainments of all its members, it is a sick society that puts productivity and performance before people. The focus on the creative process is vital for all individuals, cultures, religions, families and workplaces. It is essential that the uniqueness of individuals, families, cultures and the differences in creativity and productivity be encouraged, supported and appreciated. Equality for all the members of a society must not mean losing sight of difference. Equality entails cherishing each individual and providing opportunities to develop their giftedness and potential; it does not mean the promotion of sameness.

STARTING SCHOOL

The first day at school is a big day in every child's life. It is important that a child's first days at school are a happy experience, so that a solid foundation is set for his or her long years in school. Of course, such a foundation can easily be rocked by subsequent unpleasant experiences in school and at home. The following story typifies some of the kinds of things that have been related to me.

On the second day of school last year, a young mother rang me in a considerable state of agitation and frustration. Her story was that her son had happily started school the previous day. The following morning she noticed that he was quiet in himself and was not inclined to eat his breakfast. However, she did not become concerned until it was time for him to go to school and she could not find him. She searched the house up and down and continually called out his name – but he did not respond. Eventually, she found he had locked himself into a wardrobe and refused to emerge from it and go to school. On the phone she exclaimed: 'Will I pull him out of the wardrobe and drag him to school?' I said, 'No, he's safe in the wardrobe, so leave him there.' I knew that something threatening had happened to the child between his going and coming home from school. But I had not the faintest clue what this might have been. There were many possibilities — bullying, teasing, a teacher who was cross, critical or non-attentive, homesickness, difficulty in coping with a new situation. I also knew that if his mother made the world more emotionally unsafe by dragging him back to school then I might never discover what had upset him in the first place; there was also a major risk that he might be turned off school. What a blow that would have been to his emotional, social and educational development.

I advised his mother to reassure him that he did not have to return to school and that any time he wanted to he could come and join her downstairs. I further suggested that when he came to her she inquire gently (not interrogate) about all the things he had experienced during the previous day.

We don't talk to children enough. We tend to direct and command, but not really inquire into their world. What had happened was that the teacher, who undoubtedly had been under considerable stress, had waved a long stick over the heads of these little children when they were all seated and warned them that 'if any little boys or girls do not do what they are told, this is what they will get'. How clever of the child to seek the non-threatening environment of a wardrobe!

It is important that we do not in any way judge the teacher for her ill-advised behaviour. Next to parenting, teaching is the most difficult profession. To manage thirty or more five-year-olds is not any easy task and, in frustration, teachers can resort to authoritarian approaches to classroom management. This does not mean that their behaviour should not be challenged, but this needs to be done in an understanding and compassionate way. I believe neither parents not teachers ever deliberately neglect children, but they can do so unwittingly due to their own vulnerabilities and the stressful demands made on them.

I advised the young mother to approach the teacher, tell her the story and invite her to help make coming to school emotionally safe for her son again. The teacher was very responsive and went out of her way to welcome the child back and to create a happy and positive climate in the classroom. Within days, the boy was saying how much he loved his teacher and going to school.

There are many lessons to be learned from this child's experience, the most important being that children will love school when they are loved in school and when they come home from school. Furthermore, in these early school days, it is essential that parents and teachers watch for emotional and behavioural signs of unhappiness. Most childhood problems are due to a lack of loving in some setting or relationship or other. The cure is to restore love.

NOT SO PERFECT!

The children and adolescents who are most often referred to me for help are those who are aggressive, disruptive, violent, hyperactive, apathetic and who have lost motivation to learn. The second most referred group are children and young people who are shy, timid, fearful, school phobic, depressed and isolated. The children who are rarely referred are those who are perfectionistic, who put extreme pressure on themselves to academically (or otherwise) perform, who cannot tolerate even positive criticism or direction, and who will avoid any challenges that they feel they would not be 'tops' in. These young people tend to fret and worry around exam times, they tend to be emotionally and socially illiterate and are often isolated from their peer group. Even though they are more emotionally and suicidally at risk than their more aggressive, hyperactive, shy or timid peers, they are often the apple of their parents' and teachers' eyes. This is not surprising as they do not disrupt homes or classrooms and they bring home the prizes and achieve highly in classrooms. Nonetheless, these children need as much, if not more, help as those students who avoid or are hostile to learning. However, whilst syndromes have been created to describe children with learning problems and drugs developed to control their difficult behaviour, I know of no such investigations or professional endeavour into those children who are perfectionistic!

The signs of perfectionism are not too difficult to detect:

- Chronic fear of failure
- Addiction to success

- Long hours studying or working or practising
- Fear and fretting around examination or appraisal times
- Intolerance of even positive criticism
- Avoidance of challenges where others are likely to be better than them
- Dropping out from activities where their performance falls short of 'perfect'
- Social isolation
- Easily upset
- Thrive on success

There is a major difference between children and adults who love and enjoy academic and other activities and those who are addicted to them; the former are driven by challenge and adventure, whereas the latter are driven by fear. The fears that drive those who are pefectionistic are fear of failure, criticism and rejection.

Perfectionism in children and adults is an addiction to success. The addiction to success is very powerful and it is difficult to overcome, because, unlike other addictions (alcohol, drugs, food, smoking), those who are success-driven are reinforced strongly for their over-dedication. Perfectionism in children can give them phenomenal academic (or other, for example, sports) success, status, praise and adulation.

Where there is addiction to success, self-worth and work are strongly intertwined, and any falling short of a perfect performance can pose a serious threat to emotional and social well-being. The implication inherent in perfectionism is that 'without a perfect performance I am valueless and worthless'. It is for this very reason that these children and adults are highly at risk — even a small drop in performance can plummet them into despair or lead to their dropping out from the activity that has been their means of proving themselves in the world.

I have helped children, adolescents and young adults who dropped out of school or university because they fell short of their perfectionistic standards. I have also seen young adults who showed amazing promise at a particular sport, but dropped out for fear of not being able to maintain the high performance or following a poor display.

Probably the saddest aspect of perfectionism is the absence of deep and unconditional loving relationships: success addiction can often be an emotional desert that must subconsciously strike at the very heart of those driven to succeed. However, if you are addicted to success and you give priority to relationships, you risk the only acceptance and visibility you have known – the conditional recognition for successful performance in the 'desired' behaviour (academic or sports or domesticity or work, etc.).

Perfectionism is not a weakness, but it is a protection that seriously blocks a person's progress in life. Those who are perfectionistic have cleverly learned to gain visibility and recognition through their 'success', and this defence will be maintained until unconditionality is present – where the child or adult is cherished for self and not for what they do. The focus in helping those who are success-addicted needs to be on self-worth, not on the perfectionism. It is not wise to attempt to take a weapon away from anybody, but the need for a weapon disappears in the solid and safe world of unconditional love.

ADD – REALITY OR MYTH?

Attention Deficit Disorder (ADD) and Attention Deficit Disorder with Hyperactivity (ADDH) are psychiatric labels being pinned on children who present with a certain range of behavioural symptoms. Many of these children following diagnosis are put on Ritalin, a drug that is purported to improve attention span (although not to improve verbal ability!). The promoters of the use of Ritalin also claim that it can help children who seem to get very little out of school – who can't sit still, don't take directions well, are easily frustrated, excitable, aggressive, and have a short attention span. Wonder drug indeed! However, the research underpinning the aggressive marketing of Ritalin is very questionable.

For most children, the road to Ritalin use begins at home or in the classroom. Some medical colleagues talk about the parent who roars into the surgery with a child in one hand and a magazine or newspaper article about Ritalin or ADD or ADDH in the other, saying, 'I want you to slow my child down before I murder him'. In other cases, it is the paediatrician or family doctor who, partly in response to persuasive drug company promotion, first suggests a drug trial. But, in most instances, the initiative comes from the school. The teacher writes to the parent or calls for a parent-teacher meeting or refers the child to a school psychologist or counsellor to express her legitimate concern about a student's behaviour or academic performance, suggesting that he or she is lacking attention or is hyperactive, and recommending a psychological assessment. Most parents comply; others resist and may even change schools.

The typical list of signs of so-called ADDH are:

☐ restlessness
☐ fidgeting
☐ very short attention span, child flits from one activity to another
☐ extreme oscillations in mood
☐ clumsiness due to over-activity
☐ aggressive behaviour
☐ impulsivity in school, cannot comply with rules and has low frustration level

While children may persistently present with any of these symptoms, the presence of a 'problem' within a child should not be equated with the presence of a biological syndrome. Indeed, social and family factors may be the most significant influences on the behaviour of young children and it may be that community attention to these factors rather than the current trend of provision of extra psychiatric and behavioural-modification facilities might bring more relief to the families and schools affected and improve the quality of the lives of everybody concerned.

It is rarely the case that any one cause underlies a behavioural problem. Any assessment needs to be holistic in nature and that includes a biological evaluation as well. It is extremely worrying that ADD and ADDH are being broadcast as actual rather than hypothetical conditions. There is no biological test for these so-called syndromes, but they are implied when a certain range of behavioural symptoms are present. What is not explained is that the same range of signs can describe children with self-esteem problems, conduct disorders, emotional disorders, school phobia and mild autism. Furthermore, there is no rationale given for the fact that boys are four times more likely to be labelled than girls. Another fact is that a majority of these labelled children tend to come from disadvantaged homes compared to their better-off peers.

There is no doubt that both parenting and teaching are the most difficult professions of all. There is no training required for parenting, and teachers are not even remotely prepared to deal with the myriad of behavioural, social and emotional problems of children and their besieged parents. It does not take much common sense to realise that all the difficult behaviour said to be symptomatic of ADDH could, with equal if not more conviction and justification, be called socially deviant behaviour. In other words, the behaviour is in direct opposition to the needs of parents and teachers for compliance to certain norms, rules and standards of behaviour. Labelling children and drugging children takes some of the responsibility and stress off the shoulders of parents and teachers, but it does not resolve the reasons why children are manifesting these difficulties. It is a short-term solution for the adults; for the children it can sometimes seem as if their cry for help is being heard, but for most it leaves them labelled, drug-addicted and unhelped.

Ironically, the label Attention Deficit Disorder can be usefully applied to the adults and helping agencies who do not respond to the real needs of the labelled children. Furthermore, many of these children may be experiencing attention (love) deficit in their homes and classrooms, and what may well be needed is for these children to be loved and cherished by all who come into contact with them. Both teachers and parents need all the holistic help they can get.

MULTIPLE INTELLIGENCE: A STEP IN THE WRONG DIRECTION!

For many years, children (and adults) have been victims of a notion of intelligence that doomed them to a particular category for the whole of their lives. Typically, children were considered 'weak', 'slow', 'dull', 'below average', 'average', 'bright', 'very bright', 'superior', 'very superior', 'genius', 'gifted'. These labels arose primarily from the scoring systems of intelligence tests that placed children in a particular range of intelligence:

Severely retarded	I.Q. below 40
Moderate	I.Q. 40–59
Mild	I.Q. 60–74
Dull	I.Q. 75–89
Average	I.Q. 90–109
Bright	I.Q. 110–119
Superior	I.Q. 120–130
Very superior	I.Q. 130–140
Genius	I.Q. 140+

Children scoring in the below 40 I.Q. category generally show detectable brain damage. Curiously, most of the children scoring in the moderate category do not show any evident brain damage; however, many of them show considerable emotional and social distress. These latter distresses are not considered in the evaluation of their intelligence. Nevertheless, there is now abundant evidence that children who require special needs education are also most in need of emotional help, particularly in the areas of self-worth and family and other relationships. A healing of these areas is the launch-pad to further school learning.

The assumption is that intelligence tests measure intelligence; a further assumption is that the two major scales of an I.Q. test (verbal and performance scales) measure left and right brain intelligence. In actual fact, intelligence tests do not measure intelligence. They are an absolutely crude measure, and these tests should no longer be called intelligence tests. It is more accurate to say that I.Q. tests are measures of knowledge of a culture. For example, if you administer an I.Q. test to an Irish and an Aborigine population, the Aborigines will score extremely low on 'verbal intelligence' but score off the record on 'performance intelligence'. The Irish will score above average on the verbal scale but below average on the performance scale.

What intelligence tests measure somewhat effectively are either knowledge of a culture or differences in knowledge between two different cultures. Irish culture has become very verbally biased, whereas Aborigines are forest-dwellers and require a more performance-oriented type of knowledge to survive and thrive in their environment. It is well documented that there is no intelligence test that is culture free. What is not documented is the next logical conclusion to that fact — *that I.Q. tests are measures purely of knowledge of a culture.*

The current thinking on the notion of multiple intelligences (as opposed to the concept of global intelligence) is still based on the old philosophy of different levels of intellectual endowment, but with the added dimension of different types of intelligence. The present count is seven and comprises:

☐ Linguistic Intelligence: The capacity to use words effectively.

- Logico-Mathematical Intelligence: The capacity to use numbers effectively.
- Spatial Intelligence: The ability to perceive the visual-spatial world accurately.
- Bodily-Kinesthetic Intelligence: Expertise in using one's whole body to express ideas and feelings.
- Musical Intelligence: The capacity to perceive, discriminate, transform and express musical forms.
- Interpersonal Intelligence: The ability to perceive and make distinctions in the moods, intentions, motivations and feelings of other people.
- Intrapersonal Intelligence: Self-knowledge and the ability to act adaptively on the basis of that knowledge.

This model of seven intelligences is still regarded as a tentative formulation, and other intelligences that have been proposed include:

- Humour
- Creativity
- Culinary (cooking) ability
- Olfactory perception (sense of smell)
- Intuition
- Spirituality
- Sexuality
- Moral sensibility
- An ability to synthesise the other intelligences

The danger with the idea of multiple intelligences is that future I.Q. testing will resemble a personality test and lead to the old fixed scoring categorisations of levels of intelligence in each of the multiple intelligence categories. Children may be confined now to certain areas of knowledge because 'the test' shows where their intellectual potential lies.

It is more accurate to say that these multiple areas of intelligence represent areas of knowledge. The human psyche will keep developing new knowledge and skill areas in order to adapt to and understand the nature of the universe in which it resides. The intellectual potential to do that is always present – limitless and indefatigable. Science backs the notion of limitless capacity when it states that human beings only use one to two per cent of the billions of brain cells that they possess. How then can there be talk of levels of intelligence, or levels of different types of intelligence? It seems more logical to perceive that every human being (when no brain damage is present) possesses vast intellectual potential and that potential can be applied to developing multiple kinds of knowledge.

TO STUDY OR NOT TO STUDY

Over the years in my work with young people, I have encountered adolescent boys and girls who hate school, hate homework, do not want to be in school and can react aggressively and sometimes violently when any pressure is put upon them to study. Any attempt to outline to them the effects of their behaviour on their parents and teachers may be met with a shrug of the shoulders and a 'what do I care' verbal response. I have to be honest and say that my own immediate covert response is to want to take the young person by the scruff of the neck and tell him in no uncertain terms what I think of him and that he can think again if he thinks he can get away with his obnoxious behaviour. Thankfully, a deeper intuitive voice quickly intervenes and points out that I would be no different in behaviour from the young person were I to react in such an aggressive and oppressive way. Nevertheless, there are issues to be addressed and I would be doing no favours to myself or the unhappy parents or teachers or especially the young person, were I to ignore the situation.

There are three sets of needs to be considered: those of the student, the teachers and the parents. The approach to the student has to be one that is patient and understanding. There is no point in telling the adolescent that you 'had better get your act together' or 'grow up' or 'pull up your socks'. He will know that you are not making any attempt to understand him and that your whole purpose is to get him to conform to your wishes. The consequence is that he will dig in his heels even deeper, which will result in the parents and teachers escalating their pressure on him, and a vicious spiralling cycle will ensue. What is sure is that going down this road will bring no resolution.

It is difficult for the concerned adults to hold their nerve, as well as their temper, and to enquire 'what is it that lies behind your unwillingness to study?' Some parents see this as giving in, but no progress will be made unless the causes of the block to school and learning are unearthed. It is important for parents to be aware that sometimes the reasons may be at a subconscious level, and unless the young person feels that it is emotionally safe to break the silence on hidden causes, the reasons may even continue to be hidden from himself. In such a situation the parents need to be patient and supportive and give space and time for the deeper issues to rise to the surface of the student's mind.

I recall one adolescent initially having no idea why he hated school, study and homework, and it was only with gentle exploration that his fear of not being good enough for his father emerged. Before any progress with schoolwork could happen, what was required was resolution of his difficulties with his father. This can take time and it needs to be made very clear to the young person that in the meantime he can't be taking his problems out on other people, be it teachers, siblings, peers or parents. Any disrespect must be dealt with firmly but respectfully – this can be loss of privileges, being 'grounded', request for an apology and any sanction that provokes a responsible response.

Sometimes, even when the reasons for hating school have been detected and there has been some progress made on these issues, the young person may still persist in his notion of wanting to drop out of school and go out to work. Some parents panic and the temptation is to react by saying 'you're ruining your life and ours'. However, this brings the situation back to square one and the probability is that things will go from bad to worse. As difficult as it may be, the parents would be wise to accept the young person's stance and allow him to join the workforce. Experience is the best teacher and I have seen young people after a year of work decide to return to school.

Of course, there is the situation where the adolescent drops out of school but stays in bed all day, watches television all night and makes no effort to find a job. In such a situation, parents need to hold clear boundaries, calmly make requests for following through on the commitment he made, provide no pocket money, no meals brought to his room, no television and no being driven to recreational destinations. When parents do not stick to their guns, young people will exploit the parents' lack of resolve.

While it is important that the parents are open to listening, being understanding and supportive, mature actions from both parents and adolescents always speak louder than words. When a stalemate is reached, finding help beyond the family may be required. If the young person refuses to get help, it is vital that the parents themselves go and talk to a professional trained in family dynamics and duly inform their son or daughter of their course of action.

MAKING HOMEWORK POSITIVE

With the prospect of state, university and other school examinations on the horizon, parents tend to be more vigilant around children's application to school homework and preparation for examinations. Patience, good humour, expressions of encouragement, support and understanding are essential aspects of helping children with homework. Certainly, the absence of crossness, criticism, comparisons, cynicism, sarcasm and impatience is crucial to creating a positive environment for children to enjoy and be challenged by study. Children never become motivated when adults verbally, non-verbally (the cross face, the disapproving look, the defensive body posture) or physically hurt or threaten them. As George Bernard Shaw said a long time ago: 'You cannot cure children's problems by hurting them.'

When children hate studying and avoid it as much as they can, then patient and compassionate exploration is required to get to the reasons why they have lost interest in learning. After all, a huge percentage of adults go for the average in their lives, do not seek promotion in their jobs, avoid new challenges and new friendships, do not examine new philosophies and spiritualities and, generally, stick with what they know. These parents are in no position to inspire their children with the expansiveness, adventure and challenge of learning. It is wise for parents to check that what they request and encourage in their children is not a case of 'do as I say', but rather 'do as I do'. Children imitate the actions of adults, not their words. In any case, only 7 per cent of communication is verbal. Even before children reach any proficient use of language, they have long figured out how their parents operate in life.

It is easier on children when parents set a regular daily time for homework. Parents need to ensure that when homework is being done there are no distractions – such as television – and children will complete it more quickly. It is best that children do homework apart from each other, and there needs to be a clear rule that they do not interfere with each other during homework. If they do interrupt each other, whether by teasing, making noises or invading each other's space, then a clearly defined sanction must follow. When there are problems of self-esteem within families, children can be very cruel to each other, and it is important that parents do not let children get away with either physically or verbally abusing each other. A child's life can be made miserable if an older brother or sister dominates and controls. Parents are the ones in charge of the family, and older siblings must not be allowed to control younger children. When children are doing their homework, let them know that help is available and be sure to look in on them, giving words of praise and encouragement and perhaps a 'treat'. When homework is completed, it is important that one of the parents checks the child's effort, praises the attainment achieved and points out where the next effort needs to be focused.

Where there has been a genuine and sincere effort, even though the child may get something wrong, put the emphasis on what he or she has attained, and let the teacher shape up the next effort needed within the classroom. Do not get a child to repeat homework just because some mistakes have been made. This is very punishing for children and homework now begins to have punishing associations. It is, of course, a different situation if mistakes occur because the effort made was rushed, careless or sloppy. Then parents need to be positively firm. Finally, following homework, the best reward is always affirmation and praise, but children may also be rewarded with a favoured activity. This practice leads to children having positive associations with homework.

In carrying out these suggestions regarding homework, it is important that predictability and consistency are maintained. If parents or other childminders cannot be patient and calm with children's homework efforts and the mistakes they make, it is best that they are not involved in helping with homework.

Where children are consistently either attempting to avoid homework or are overdiligent and even scrupulous, these need to be recognised as signs of avoidance, hostility and perfectionism and as revelations of self-esteem difficulties. Attention to the child's self-esteem is then a priority.

PSYCHOLOGICAL ABSENCE IN EDUCATION

At a time when Ireland's educational shortcomings are being highlighted by our European partners, the risks to Irish society need to be seriously contemplated. Recent OECD comparisons have placed Ireland among the weakest in terms of reading standard at age fourteen; 20 per cent of Irish students show literacy problems compared to 5 per cent in France and Finland.

These figures prompted the suggestion by Fine Gael that potential drop-outs from second-level schools be paid approximately €45 weekly to stay in school. Though well-intentioned, the proposal is a worryingly misguided plan for a number of reasons:

- It does not address the issue of why such a high percentage of students are not attaining literacy and numeracy.
- It assumes that physical presence in the classroom ensures that learning takes place.
- It ignores the finding that extrinsic rewards are rarely effective carrots.
- It does not consider that the discriminating practice of rewarding the poorly motivated and disadvantaged may affect those students who are intrinsically motivated.
- It puts pressure on an already highly stressed teaching profession to teach students who do not want to be in school.

As regards the first issue raised above, there are multiple reasons why a good percentage of students drop out early, and money is unlikely to resolve those causes, which include:

- Conflictual home environment
- Parents' own poor level of educational attainment
- Parents' negative attitudes to education
- Push from family to get work
- Peers' negative attitudes to school
- Lack of role models in local community
- Students/parents not seeing education as an option
- Student's poor self-esteem
- Run-down and demeaning school environment
- School curriculum not geared towards particular student's needs
- Teaching approach not suitable for particular student
- Problems within the student (hunger, drug-taking, fatigue)
- Humiliating circumstances of having fallen so far behind other students
- The home address and accent factors – what's the point?
- Lack of integration of educational initiatives to help the disadvantaged
- Lack of guidance

In view of the above list it would be better if the proposed £100 million was spent more creatively. Some possible spending could be on evaluation of current interventions, development of a mentoring system, creative linking of education and work, ways of raising these young people's sense of themselves, fostering of a love of learning and whole-family educational interventions.

One of the principal oversights of the Educational Youth Wage proposal is the assumption that physical presence in the classroom is a guarantee of educational progress and consequent reduction in educational disadvantage. One of the major sources of stress in teaching is not the physical but the psychological absence of children in the classroom.

A high percentage of children occupy their attention with issues that may be far more important to them than the school curriculum. Examples of what occupies their minds other than academic learning are:

- Worries about a troubled parent
- Anxiety regarding going home after school
- Fears of being bullied
- Preoccupation with abuse experiences
- How to get attention of peers
- How to get noticed by teachers
- Dislike of self
- Worries about physical appearance
- Hunger
- Planning how to get or make some money
- Daydreaming
- Occupied with own interests (for example, sports, art, music)
- Fatigue

Many children who do not concentrate on their studies are often inappropriately labelled as having ADD (Attention Deficit Disorder) or as lazy or possessing poor intellect. More often than not what is missing is a holistic assessment of these students' learning difficulties.

It is essential that the causes of psychological absence be addressed before aggravating the problem with enforced or cajoled physical presence in the classroom. Psychological readiness for learning is not sufficiently addressed in schools, but teachers well know the frustration of trying to teach children who are not motivated. Efforts to resolve these children's emotionally, socially and physically disadvantaged worlds would be money well spent.

POSITIVE SELF-TALK AND EXAMINATIONS

Given the amount of challenges that adolescents have to face, they need all the help and support they can get. One of the greatest challenges they will face is the pressure of an unfair and competitive state examination system. A very useful skill to teach adolescents and children is positive self-talk. There are teachers, team coaches, managers and political leaders who can verbally motivate their charges into responsible efforts, commitment and excitement around a particular challenge. There is nothing to stop individuals being an inspiring influence on themselves by using positive rhetoric to spur them on to greater learning efforts.

It is very helpful for children to learn how critical self-talk leads to worry, anxiety, fear and anger, and consequently makes learning and facing examinations difficult. Typical examples of children's limiting self-talk are:

- 'I'm useless at remembering.'
- 'I'm not clever enough to understand that subject.'
- 'I'm the slowest in the class.'
- 'I hate doing my homework.'
- 'Examinations are totally unfair.'
- 'I'm afraid of failing.'
- 'School is boring.'

It needs to be understood that critical statements are revelations of self-esteem difficulties and as such immediately indicate the need for steps to be taken by parents and teachers to elevate the child's self-esteem. While helping children to feel good about themselves and have a sense of their unlimited intellectual potential is far more important than the attempt to alter the above pessimistic statements, helping children to alter such self-talk does include them in the process of feeling better about themselves.

Self-statements that would counter the 'put down' statements in the examples above might be:

- □ 'I have limitless memory capacity.'
- □ 'There is no limit to my intellectual power to understand things.'
- □ 'I am unique and different and my way of learning is unique to me, as it is for each person.'
- □ 'Homework is a challenge and a responsibility that I am happy to take on.'
- □ 'Examinations are challenging and I'm determined to do my utmost, without having to prove myself to anyone.'
- □ 'The only real failure is when people give up doing something.'
- □ 'School is my stepping-stone to wider choices to living my life.'

Positive self-talk always needs to be realistic, with the young person accepting present limitations and retaining love and belief in self. It can be very useful for students during examinations to prepare positive self-statements for different stages of the examination process:

- □ before the examination
- □ at the beginning of the examination
- □ during the examination
- □ when feeling panicky
- □ after the examination

Examples of such positive self-statements include:

- □ 'I am determined to stay relaxed and put my best effort into doing the examination.'
- □ 'I am going to read the examination paper calmly and confidently.'
- □ 'I am going to concentrate on the question I'm doing and nothing else.'
- □ 'It's okay to feel nervous now and I'm just going to breathe deeply, let go of tension as I exhale and put my focus back on just doing my best.'
- □ 'It's over now, I did my best and right now I want to move to my next planned activity – no post-mortems!'

Positive self-talk is not a magical formula; the real magic is for students to accept their unique selves, have a sense of their limitless intelligence and know that examinations are no measure of their worth and value. Nevertheless, practice of positive self-talk does help. It certainly has a far stronger effect when it is infused with feelings of conviction and solid enthusiasm.

Parents and teachers can be a great source of support to students facing examinations, by being affirming, supportive and encouraging. At all costs they need to avoid the use of criticism, cajoling, manipulation, cynicism, sarcasm and any behaviour that lessens a child's belief in self and makes learning and examinations threatening experiences. Comparisons with others or competition with other schools or siblings or cousins also need to be avoided. The best form of competition is self-competition – this is far more productive in generating enthusiasm for learning and a calmer response to formal evaluations.

SELF-OBSERVATION: THE KEY TO TEACHING

There has been much discussion about professional accountability within the teaching profession. There has been talk of publishing the state examination records of individual schools as a measure of the effectiveness of a school's teaching. However, such a measure is crude and takes no account of what real teaching is all about: giving students the cognitive and career skills they need, helping students to learn about themselves so that they are able to live peacefully with themselves and with others, and helping students to develop into mature, competent and self-motivated adults. Furthermore, certain schools may have a group of students attending from a particular middle-class culture, for example, whose parents are predominantly in the professional career category. In such schools, stimulation, emphasis on academic achievement, motivation and financial resources may be higher than in schools in less advantaged areas.

Certainly, professional accountability becomes expedient when individual teachers and schools are neither personally nor organisationally accountable. Presently, such phenomena are very evident in the political field. My own belief is that the most effective form of accountability is self-observation; this coupled with each school observing its own culture would guarantee a high degree of responsible behaviour.

Self-observation would entail a teacher regularly going through a checklist of behaviours that are the hallmarks of being an effective teacher and determining where strengths and challenges lie. Any shortcomings would provide the opportunity for further professional and personal development. A crucial requirement would be that the culture of the school would accept shortcomings in a positive way and would not make it threatening for a teacher to identify and seek help and support on a particular professional incompetence. There are many teachers who live in fear of judgment and condemnation and are therefore forced to cover up areas of teaching where they are less than competent.

A competency teaching list could include the following:

- Do I like students?
- Do I respect students?
- Do I address students by their first names?
- Am I challenged by teaching?
- Do I respond to failure and success as equal and integral parts of teaching?
- Do I put the emphasis on learning as an adventure and not as a pressure to perform?
- Do I positively correct students' homework?
- Do I arrive on time for class?
- Do I have definite boundaries around respect for self and others?
- Do I communicate directly and clearly what is required of students in and out of the classroom?
- Do I listen to students?
- Am I firm and do I take definitive action when violations of the rights of teachers and students occur?
- Do I maintain understanding for the student who presents classroom difficulties whilst being clear that his or her problem behaviours cannot be allowed to be sources of violations of other people's rights?
- Do I seek back-up support when needed?

☐ Do I liaise with parents at the early signs of difficulties?
☐ Is my sense of self separate from what I do?
☐ Does my teaching approach inspire or threaten children?
☐ Do I accept and celebrate the uniqueness and individuality of each student?
☐ When under stress do I seek solutions?

The above list is by no means exhaustive and it would be advisable for teachers to devise their own checklist to reflect the responsibilities that are peculiar to their own school setting. Nevertheless, there are common issues that all teachers need to address in evaluating their teaching style; these revolve around their own sense of self, their attitude to education and to failure and success, their cooperation with management and fellow members of staff, their relationships with students and parents and their response to children's learning efforts and difficulties.

It would benefit teachers for parents and students to be aware of the above list of responsibilities, so that parents, in particular, could support teachers to meet their obligations. When parents (and students) observe a falling short of what is desirable, it is incumbent on them to confront the teacher and request that the teacher take on the challenges to improving competency. In the same way that an individual student's emotional and behavioural difficulties cannot be allowed to block or violate the rights of other students and teachers, so too the shortcomings of teachers cannot become a block to students' learning and emotional and social development. Confrontation is an act of caring and its purpose is not to judge or to blame, but to provide an opportunity for ongoing professional development that can benefit all in the school system, particularly the teacher who is challenged.

THE CARING SCHOOL

Every social system has a unique culture, and its nature can have a profound influence on its members. No two schools are alike and, indeed, no two classrooms have the same atmosphere. Sadly, there are some schools or classrooms that darken the presence of their members and profoundly affect students' and teachers' innate love of learning. Equally, there are schools that inspire children, and indeed teachers, to retain their natural curiosity, eagerness and love of learning, and these environments can have a life-long positive influence on children.

Every social system has a duty to ensure that its members are cherished, challenged and fairly treated. The architects of a social system are the leaders, and in this regard school principals and school managers have the responsibility of developing a caring school system that promotes the total welfare of all members of the school. However, leaders cannot accomplish this task without the responsible and respectful cooperation of the other members of the school. It would be wise for managers, principals and teachers to consider parents as major contributors to the culture of a school and any marginalising of parents as detrimental to the school's culture. When a principal or school manager falls short of this responsibility, it becomes incumbent on others staff members, parents and students to demand the establishment of a caring culture.

Every school comprises the individual presence of each person and the collective presence of all the members of the school. School cultures, like all cultures, are difficult to define. They are not easily discerned; what you see is not what it is all about. One of the major difficulties with a school culture is that each classroom can also be a culture within itself and may not reflect the pattern of the wider school culture. In a situation where the school culture lessens the presence of its members, sometimes an individual teacher's classroom can be an oasis in the desert of an uncaring school culture. However, where the opposite situation occurs, confusion and frustration can reign, and students, in particular, can become distressed because of the lack of consistency in caring, respect and definite, fair boundaries. Other teachers can also become resentful at the uncooperative and deleterious influence of those teachers who prove resistant to any demands for cooperative behaviour. To date, strong measures have not tended to be employed to bring about harmony in the school culture, but this is neglectful, not only of those in distress, but also of the teachers who are the source of the distress.

One wonders what children think of adult values when day in and day out they are exposed to behaviours that seriously lessen their presence in the classroom. Parents have told me of teachers who are critical, sarcastic, cynical, who shout and roar, and of the children who dread or feel sick at the thought of going to school. Sometimes these parents defend their non-confrontation of the untenable situation by claiming 'the child will have a lovely teacher next year'. Sadly, by then the child's fear of school, teachers and learning may have become a solid defense against being in school.

It is equally true to say that no teacher should have to face daily into a classroom where either an individual student or group of students are disruptive, aggressive, uncooperative and sometimes violent. There is something radically wrong with a school culture and the wider cultures of community and the Department of Education when these behaviours go unchallenged. Whether we like it or not, each one of us is in some way responsible when any member of a social system is negligent or neglected.

Whilst each school culture is a unique phenomenon, there are certain fundamental aspects to all caring school cultures:

- Person–centred (rather than programme-centred)
- Relationships seen as priority
- Learning and teaching known to be directly related to how student and teacher view self respectively
- Presence and absence of each school member matters
- Discipline system for all (not just students)
- Group decision-making
- Emphasis on educational effort rather than academic performance
- Mistakes and failures seen as opportunities for learning (not criticism)
- Success and failure viewed as relative terms
- Belief in each member's unique giftedness and limitless potential
- Intelligence and knowledge seen as separate issues
- Learning to have only positive associations
- Listening to the needs of all members
- Back-up support system to deal with neglect of any member
- Openness to change
- Freedom to be different
- Management style that is transformational in nature

The above list is by no means exhaustive, but implementation of these recommendations would go a long way to creating a school environment that reaches out with heart and mind to all its members.

PART FOUR
SELF

- ☐ Care of self
- ☐ Be yourself
- ☐ Clarifying self-worth and self-esteem
- ☐ Beauty is in the eye of the beheld
- ☐ Once bitten, twice shy
- ☐ New Ireland, new challenges
- ☐ Where are the men?
- ☐ Living in the light

CARE OF SELF

Architects of social systems (the family, school, classroom, community, church, workplace) have a responsibility to make time for self. Parents, teachers, managers, clergy, community leaders and politicians have a sacred duty to be there for themselves, to respect, love, honour and take responsibility for their own unique being. In practical terms this means being affirming of themselves, taking good care of their physical selves, listening to their own voices, identifying their needs, being in touch with their feelings, valuing all of their emotions and, when necessary, talking them out in full openness. Care for self also involves rest, rest, rest, time for reflection, acting out spontaneously from your real self and not being controlled by others. It is essential that these social architects live their own lives so that they are in the free position to encourage their charges to be true to themselves.

Loving self is a difficult challenge as we are only beginning to emerge from social systems that darkened human presence. Anonymity is still common for many adult members of family, school, church, political and work cultures. In the words of Nelson Mandela: 'Our deepest fear is that we are powerful beyond measure. It is our light, not our darkness, that we fear most.' The more people who take up the challenge of embracing and expressing their sacred and unique worth, the easier it will become for leaders to take 'the road less travelled'.

The road most travelled continues to be the one of fear, dependence, addictions to work, caring, success, competitiveness, dominance, control, jealousy, possessiveness, depression, ostracisation, intellectual and social snobbery and hyper-sensitivity to criticism.

There are many adults who have a deep fear of taking any time for self. These people are addicted to caring, and it can often be more difficult to take a caring behaviour away from a person who compulsively cares than it is to take a drink away from an alcoholic. Regrettably, people who over-care for others make others helpless as a result of their need for others to remain dependent on them. Any attempt to become independent of the parent, partner or other who overprotects may result in the threatening reactions of sulking, withdrawal, guilt-inducing responses of 'after all I've done for you', rejection and hostility. The temptation to return to the status quo 'for peace sake' serves neither the giver nor the receiver of care. There is nothing enlightened about shrinking so that another will not feel threatened by you. When the receiver of overprotection maintains their bid for freedom, there is a strong possibility that the person who lives her or his life through caring will hear the permission to care and begin to give time to self. The other eventual benefit is that a mature adult-adult relationship will emerge so that caring is mutual, responsibility lies with self and each person can be authentic.

Then there are those who dominate others so that they consistently make time for them, and these people will ridicule any attempt to be separate from them. This is not dissimilar to overprotection, except that the condition for acceptance is 'you must always be there for me' rather than 'I must always be there for you'. The hidden messages behind these condi-tional ways of relating are respectively: 'I am nothing, so you must live your life for me', and 'I am nothing, so I will live my life for you'. The absence of any sense of self is blatantly and sadly apparent. The dominating social architect is as anonymous to self as the overprotective one. Each of them has a sacred responsibility to journey inwards and discover their own individuality, wonder and identity. Only by taking on this process will they be able to disengage from their enmeshed relationships with others. Furthermore, it is in achieving their possession of self and separateness from others that they will be in a position to mirror the worth and separateness of those for whom they have leadership responsibilities.

Whilst the majority of social architects are either those who are over-there for others, not for self, or make others be over-there for them but are not there for self or others, there is a tragic minority whose presence has been so darkened that they do not permit themselves even a glimmer of worthiness. These individuals are so alienated from self that they neither give to nor expect to receive from others. Their lifestyle reflects their interior blackness: avoidance of all challenges, apathy, hopelessness, despair, lovelessness, isolation and neglect of physical and emotional welfare, addictions to alcohol or drugs, or, conversely, extreme drive, ambition or work addiction.

Staying on the road inwards requires discipline, patience and support from others. As regards the latter, it helps to surround yourself with people who are life-giving, rather than life-taking. Join courses and groups that are dynamic and progressive and that affirm the worthiness and vast capability of each person. Remember that embracing your own worthiness is not an act of selfishness and it is not narcissism; contrary to what we are told, protective obsessions arise from not loving self but rather from the fierce need to make others love us.

BE YOURSELF

Intimacy with self and others is good for your health. Numerous studies have shown that closeness with self and others significantly extends life expectancy, boosts immune function, protects against disease and speeds up recovery time after surgery. One long-term prospective study that followed a group of 5,000 individuals over a thirty-five year period found that those who did not have close relationships with their parents in childhood died two to three times earlier than those who felt loved and wanted. The researchers also found that over 90 per cent of the 'unloved' group had one or more diagnosed illnesses such as heart disease, cancer, ulcers, blood pressure and alcohol dependence, compared to 45 per cent of the 'loved' group. It has also been shown time and time again that people who feel lonely, depressed, alienated and isolated are more likely to suffer illness or die prematurely. What is needed for health is closeness and support. This does not necessarily mean sexual intimacy. Such platonic love can be with friends, family, colleagues and even with strangers.

However, to reach out to others as an adult you need first of all to be able to reach into self. A strong sense of your interiority is the solid ground from which nobody can dismiss, exile or demean you. Such inner regard for self is also the platform from which you can reach out to others. Essentially your present sense of interiority will determine your exteriority. As a psychologist I know that I can only help an individual to reach the same level of development that I have attained myself. When we do not have a sense of our own worthiness to love and be loved, it is far too threatening to reach out with heart and mind to others. Indeed, each of us has a profound duty to come into the light of our worth so that our presence automatically liberates others to give and receive closeness.

Social scientists believe that the emphasis by psychologists on individuality blocks a basic drive for support and connection. I have heard it voiced by church leaders that 'individuality has destroyed the family'. However, the social scientists and some clergy appear to be confusing individuality with individualism. *Individuality* is about the expression of your real and authentic self. The words of Shakespeare express this well: 'To thine own self be true, and as sure as night follows day thou canst not then be false to any man.' *Individualism*, on the other hand, is a form of egocentricity whereby people act as if the world revolves around them; these individuals can neither give nor truly receive love. Such people are extremely demanding, but their thirst for recognition and acceptance is a bottomless well that is impossible to fill. Deep down they feel unloved and are not in a place to give love. As children, these individuals would have been 'spoilt' by parents who gave them everything they demanded. Their parents would never have encouraged them to be separate, independent, or to express their uniqueness and giftedness. Even though they would have been the 'centre' of attention, they were not allowed to centre on themselves, but learned cleverly to respond to the needs of parents to live their lives through them or offset intimacy by material giving. As adults, they will attempt to compel and manipulate others into being there for them. There is another form of individualism, which is less obvious, but just as insidious. This is the attainment of recognition by wanting others to always need you, and any attempt by them to become independent will be greeted with withdrawal, hostile silences, sulking and rejection.

Love is a two-sided coin; it is about both giving and receiving and its focus is on the sacredness and uniqueness of the person. While the focus of individualism is on behaviour rather than the person, the focus of individuality is on the person. Unconditional love is possible only when the person is seen as worthy of both receiving and giving love. There are no behavioural strings to such intimacy. In this way individuality is the cornerstone of intimacy and connectedness with others. The extent of your own regard for yourself will be the measure of your relationship with others.

There are many people who live in interior darkness, and unless they are helped and supported to switch on the light of their unique worth, they will remain in a place of dis-ease and create unsupportive relationships with others.

A groundswell whereby many people make the journey inwards is needed to lighten the task, the duty to love self and others. It has to be seen that these duties go hand in hand and both processes need to be encouraged, supported and celebrated. The Catholic culture kept secret our most sacred duty to love self and, as a result, made it impossible for people to love others. The darkness of that culture is being revealed daily by the sad revelations of sexual, physical and emotional abuse. We must learn and grow from these experiences and be determined that the solid foundation of love of self and others will not allow such neglect to occur again.

The wonder, uniqueness, goodness, individuality and genius of each child and adult needs to be affirmed in all of the social systems they inhabit. It is both an individual and collective responsibility to ensure regard, respect and equality for each person. Every social system must particularly guard against anonymity of any of its members, ensure that no double standards exist and that some individuals, by virtue of their position, are not seen as more important than others. Status, riches or education do not increase the worthiness of people, but there are many who believe that they do, and the consequence is a snobbery that demeans others. Worthiness lies in your person, not in your behaviour. Behaviour, achievements and possessions are only experiences that come and go, but making them the measure of your worth only darkens your own presence and that of others.

There are some who may defensively reject the above as being spiritually based, but I believe that love of self and others is essential, practical and expedient if we are to live in harmony with each other.

The giving and receiving of unconditional love is not a benign issue that we can choose to ignore. On the contrary, it is vital for our total well-being because mind and body are indivisible. Eastern medicine and progressive Western medicine believes that each cell in your body communicates with all the other cells to enable the body to work as a unit. In effect, how you communicate emotionally inside and outside yourself will largely determine the cellular activities of your body.

Nurturing closeness with self and others involves:

- Unconditional acceptance of self and others.
- Giving and receiving warmth, tenderness and affection without any covert or overt manipulation.
- Being with people who love self, others and life.
- Finding a supportive, family-friendly workplace.
- Having people to talk to about your innermost needs, feelings and conflicts.

- A balanced lifestyle.
- Practising loving kindness towards each person you meet, whether partner, friend, colleague, relative or stranger.

Your health is one of your most important investments and the maintenance of closeness with self and others is the key. Regrettably, having has become the sinister enemy of intimacy and physical well-being.

CLARIFYING SELF-WORTH
AND SELF-ESTEEM

There tends to be confusion in our understanding of the concepts of self-worth and self-esteem, often leading to misguided helping.

Self-worth is a given, unchangeable; it is what you are from the moment of conception: sacred, worthy of giving and receiving love, unique, individual, possessing vast intellectual potential and giftedness. Self-worth cannot be damaged or taken from you; it is always there, but for many people it lies hidden behind defensive walls. Your self-worth has to do with your unique being, and no behaviour either adds or takes from your person. It is when the person of a child or adult begins to be seen through his or her behaviour that self-esteem emerges as a protection against not being loved and valued for self.

Self-esteem is a screen self, a crust you form around your real self in order to survive in the social system of which you are a member, or in particular relationships. The greater the threats to your expression of your self-worth, the lower is your self-esteem and the higher are your protectors. Basically, self-esteem is the amount of your real self that you dare show to people. It is in this sense that self-esteem is a screen, because it hides or veils what would be threatening to reveal. For example, each child is unique, individual and different. However, difference has not been affirmed and celebrated in Irish culture, where children (and adults) conform to the demand to be the same in homes, classrooms, churches, communities and sports fields. The word 'conform' illustrates powerfully how self-esteem is developed as a shadow, a veil over what would be threatening to show – difference. 'Con' means 'false' and 'form' means 'image'. To conform makes you create a false image, a shadow self that hides the aspect(s) of real self that is not accepted.

The more characteristics of your true self that are not affirmed, or, on appearance, are severely punished and violated, the greater the defensive screen created by the person. There are individuals who describe themselves, for example, as 'stupid', 'evil', 'vile', 'ugly', 'unlovable', 'hateful', 'bad'. These persons created these self-esteem defences as a means of survival and, not surprisingly, it takes considerable patience on the part of others to help these individuals to let go of their shadow selves.

There is a certain joy and comfort in being hidden, as it reduces further exposure to rejection and neglect, but what a disaster not to come to a place of being able to fully express your sacred, unique and amazing presence.

There is an inverse relationship between your level of self-esteem and your level of protectors. For instance, if your early experiences were of a loveless and harsh nature, you would emerge from childhood with low self-esteem and with remarkably high protectors. The person with low self-esteem may either be very aggressive, violent, blaming, workaholic, alcohol dependent, possessive, or be extremely passive, withdrawn, apathetic, drug-addicted, shy, timid, fearful and depressed.

Many people fall into the arena of having middle self-esteem, where they hide only some aspects of their true selves and where their defensive manoeuvres are moderate in nature. A person with middle self-esteem may say of himself: 'I'm not all bad', 'I'm your average man', 'I'm as good as the next person', 'There are people worse that me'. His protectors would either be being argumentative, inflexible, over-ambitious, hypersensitive to criticism or being dependent, fearful, anxious, uncertain, tentative and concerned about how others see him. Nevertheless, those with middle self-esteem are much closer to their self-worth than those with low self-esteem.

People with high self-esteem, which accounts for about 5 to 10 per cent of the population, are very close to the full expression of their unique presence and worth, but because we live in a world where the threats to being truly yourself are frequent, intense and enduring, some small level of protection is required. Nevertheless, people with high self-esteem are those who work out mostly from their immutable self-worth and hence are loving, capable of receiving love, spontaneous, unique, different, individual, expansive, adventurous, creative and fearless.

It is important to understand that self-esteem arises in response to threats to the true expression of self and is an amazing and creative defense by those children and adults whose self-worth is threatened. Change can only begin with the acceptance of the shadow self as being a necessary 'evil'; such embracing of your present level of self-esteem is the first step on the journey back to your real self. Stanislavsky, the Russian dramatist and thinker, wrote: 'The longest and most exciting journey is the journey inwards.'

BEAUTY IS IN THE EYE OF THE BEHELD

According to new research, the percentage of people – both women and men – who are dissatisfied with their bodies has more than doubled in the past two decades. This may be due to the fact that we are bombarded with media images that hold up an impossible ideal. Of course, it may also be due to the fact that more people are voicing their dissatisfaction with their bodies compared to twenty years ago when vanity was socially and religiously ridiculed. However, there is no doubt that the present preoccupation with the 'body beautiful' adds to the pressure of looking good.

Sensitivity about one's appearance can range from low to extreme. Those in the low to moderate range of sensitivity are critical of some aspect of their appearance, but, generally speaking, they manage with the help of grooming and cosmetics to feel fairly comfortable in social situations. Those in the high to extreme range tend to hate their bodies and either spend endless hours in front of the mirror or avoid the mirror altogether; they dread social situations and may even become socially phobic.

The sad and fascinating aspect of people who are critical of their physicality is that even when they are judged as 'beautiful' or hailed as 'screen goddesses', their own internal image of themselves blocks the reception of any positive feedback on their bodies. It is in this sense that beauty is *not* in the eye of the beholder, but in the eye of the beheld. Individuals with doubts about their physical attractiveness either want constant reassurance of their beauty (bottomless pit) or hate when any comments, either positive or negative, are made. Indeed, some individuals can become dangerously aggressive towards others or themselves when a critical remark is made. Paranoia can often accompany rejection of one's body. For example, if a person suffering from this anxiety believes herself to be overweight and someone looks at her in a shop or restaurant or at work, she will automatically think that she is being talked about or laughed at. This is known as projection, whereby the person who is vulnerable transfers her own doubts about herself into the thoughts and actions of another. It is a wonderful protective mechanism, as it leads to avoidance of others so that no real rejection can occur.

The fear of rejection develops out of earlier experiences of rejection as a child. Many of us suffered negative comments about our bodies as children, or experienced other children being seen as more attractive. My own abiding memory is the comment that 'maybe someday you'll be as good-looking as your brother'! I have worked with men and women who were labelled 'fat', 'monkey-faced', 'plain', 'short', 'lanky', 'ugly'. These criticisms came from adults and other children. Adolescents can be particularly nasty to each other regarding physical appearance.

Specialists in body image suggest ways of overcoming the problem by accentuating the positive, identifying and challenging your critical thinking patterns and learning to receive compliments. The problem with accentuating the positive is that you are discriminating against certain parts of your body in favour of other parts. You will be unable to find a mature acceptance of yourself in this way. Each person's body is unique in shape, size, height, colour, hair, posture, etc. Not only is your body unique, it is also sacred and carries every precious aspect of your being. It is only through embracing and accepting your physical difference from all others that you can find security in your physical presence. Being compared to someone else is an act of rejection and a loss of possession of your sacred presence.

The difficulty in receiving compliments will only change when you honour your own unique physical presence: an external message is only accepted when it matches the internal one. Furthermore, criticising yourself for taking notice of criticism by others will cease only in the full embrace of your own deep acceptance of your unique physical presence. Physical care of self flows from such acceptance.

ONCE BITTEN, TWICE SHY

Social phobia is common to all ages and can seriously block a person's emotional, social and occupational progress. Individuals who complain of this condition dread being the focus of attention and will do anything to avoid such situations. Depending on the intensity of the phobia, even being with friends can be a threatening experience. A high percentage of adolescents experience debilitating shyness, but as their identity formation develops they tend to feel more confident and less threatened by social events. However, there are a sizeable number of adolescents whose social fears persist into adulthood, and more often than not these fears have endured from early childhood. Once the fear of public embarrassment takes hold, these individuals feel powerless to think or reason their way out of panic. Emotion is always stronger than reason.

Children are not born shy but they cleverly learn to develop shyness and timidity to offset humiliation, criticism and rejection. Shyness is not a problem but rather a weapon against being hurt. I've helped many young and older individuals with social difficulties, where I've placed the focus not on their shyness but on the expression of their unique presence and the development of independence of others. Many of these individuals have told me of experiences of being embarrassed and ridiculed in front of people. When I quote to them the saying 'once bitten, twice shy' and ask them 'how often have you been bitten?' the answer is often 'several hundred times'. The strength of shyness and timidity is its power to reduce judgment by others. Ask yourself how you treat somebody who presents as shy and timid. The reply is 'with kid gloves'; now who is controlling whom?

The typical signs of social phobia are:

- Blushing
- Poor eye contact
- Hunched posture
- Stammering
- Physical shaking
- Heart palpitations
- Stomach butterflies
- Panic attacks
- Avoidance of certain or all social events

When asked why they dread socialising, people with a social phobia may give any of a number of explanations:

- I can't stand being the centre of attention
- I'm afraid I'll blush
- I'm afraid of fainting
- I'm afraid of making a fool of myself
- I'm afraid of being rejected

When you consider that the most common phobia of all is the fear of public speaking, it makes sense that social phobia is also quite common. Ninety per cent of people dread public speaking for precisely the same reasons given above for shyness. However, while you can go through life without having to speak in public, it is not possible to live your life without meeting people.

What typically underlines a social phobia is poor sense of self, dependence on others for approval and a conviction that whatever you do or say, you are going to be rejected outright. Your protection is to reject yourself before others even have a chance of rejecting you. The causes inevitably lie in early experiences where you were rejected or humiliated when you displayed a behaviour that did not meet the approval of others. Examples would be clinging, crying, blushing, being overweight, fainting, failure, stress.

Drug companies offer many 'miracle' drugs for shyness. Whilst I have no difficulty with short-term medication to give people in such social distress an edge to overcome their shyness, what these individuals most need to do is to come to a place of acceptance of self, to cease defining themselves through their behaviour and to become independent of the approval of others. Basically what is required for individuals who have been bitten and are several hundred times shy is not to care whether or not they blush, shake, trip, fall, faint or stammer; they need to learn that their behaviour is just a way of experiencing the world and neither adds nor detracts from their worth. When such a process proves difficult it is wise to seek psychosocial help.

NEW IRELAND, NEW CHALLENGES

In the pluralist society and economic prosperity of the 'new' Ireland, not only are parents expected to be up-to-date in designer fashion and current-year registered cars, they are expected to have dynamic and well-paid jobs, be available at all times for work and family concerns on their mobile phones, be sexually active and 'with it', be in touch with their feelings and the feelings and concerns of their children, have high self-esteem, provide for their children's education (often up to the age of twenty-five) and be on hand for their children. Quite a tall order for a parent who may work a minimum of eight hours a day outside the home and as many hours inside the home. Mothers still carry 90 per cent of domestic and parenting responsibilities. Fathers or partners often work twelve-hour days and that does not include commuting time. It is getting increasingly difficult to get experienced and trained childminders, so that working parents frequently have to deal with the fall-out from the emotional under-involvement and limited parenting skills of some childminders.

Another product of the 'success' culture is that some parents resort to bribing their children with expensive holidays or designer outfits or money for high academic performance, sometimes as early as primary school. Such behaviour stems from the parents' own subconscious addiction to success. I recall a young woman who had a profound spiritual experience during a weekend retreat, but when I enquired if this would mean that she would now give more time to spirituality, she replied: 'I don't think I have had enough materialism yet'! It is difficult for people to resist the over-whelming tide of materialism that exists today, but there is a danger that 'having will become the sinister enemy of being'.

The cornerstone of effective parenting is being in touch with your own sacred self, your uniqueness, individuality, vast capability and inherent goodness. This can only be experienced fully in the stillness of 'not doing', in the power of emptiness, where you touch into your real worth, which is separate from what you do. Equally, being there in a similar way for partner and children is central to effective, enduring and fulfilling relationships. There is nothing more powerful than the love that is communicated in the silent embrace of another.

There is no doubt that many parents are concerned about the new, different and materialistic pace of Irish life. They are acutely aware that there is less time to listen to and talk to children, and they are worried about teenage sex, teenage pregnancies and the ever-increasing academic competitiveness that children are facing. Parents also have anxieties about getting the best education and career prospects for their children. Furthermore, they are rightly concerned about the effects of the rising level of marital and family breakdown on children. These concerns are worthy of attention and, as in all aspects of parenting, parents firstly need to address themselves.

I do not want to be a success spoilsport. On the contrary, we deserve to celebrate the fruits of our labours and our emergence from an oppressive political and religious history, where we protected ourselves by being inferior. There is now a real surge of power in the Celtic psyche where the Irish in the world are seen as models for business acumen, drive, ambition and political and social progress, with a long list of achievements in the arenas of music, sports and literature. However, we must guard against swinging into superiority, and we must realise that the power we are discovering in ourselves is in everyone. We must also remember that love is vital for human life and that a successful economic and progressive culture that loses sight of that fundamental value will eventually collapse in on itself. In homes, schools, workplaces, communities and churches, the celebration, respect and valuing of the sacredness of each human being must not be swallowed up by the wave of success.

Parents and leaders, in particular, need to model a lifestyle that is balanced and that places priority on the care and love of self and others. They also need to demonstrate the expansiveness of life, keep a good sense of humour and show that life is an adventure and not a trial.

WHERE ARE THE MEN?

Recently I was giving a talk and workshop at an ISPCC conference on Violence and Children. Several hundred people attended the conference; 95 per cent of them were female. I asked the women in the audience: 'Where are the men?' The answer I got was: 'At home minding the children.' Given the nature of the conference topic, I was tempted to say that it would have been more desirable if the women had stayed home on this occasion and encouraged and supported the men to attend the conference. There is no suggestion here that women do not perpetuate violence, but it is a common phenomenon that men do not attend conferences, lectures and courses on personal development, relationships and child rearing.

Violence is still a predominantly male problem. One in five women are still subjected to physical assaults by men. Forty per cent of workers experience verbal and physical bullying in the workplace, mainly perpetrated by males. The most frequent cause of death in the workplace in America is murder. Violence is still commonplace and, regrettably, only lightly sanctioned on the sports field. Many men, and a sizeable percentage of women, still believe that the way to discipline children is by slapping them. What is even more astounding is that a lot of men project responsibility for their violent actions onto others, and say that if they were not pressurised they would not physically react! It is essential that men and women own their violent behaviour and see that it is in their own hands to choose or not to choose violence. They have a duty to learn more respectful and effective ways of coping with pressure.

Certainly over the last two decades women have made considerable progress in realising their own worth, communicating more directly and clearly, demanding equality in the home and workplace and having a stronger voice in the community and churches. Whilst there is a long road yet to travel on the attainment of gender equality in the home, church and workplace, women are miles ahead of men in personal and social development. It is mostly women who now blow the whistle on unhappy relationships. Women are also learning to exist without men; this is manifested in the unprecedented rise in single parenting, single life and choosing to live with a female rather than a male partner.

Sadly, men remain imprisoned in their 'macho' world and exhibit major fears about revealing the inner world of their feelings, the expression of intimacy and the acceptance of vulnerability. No matter what psychosocial topic I and my colleagues give seminars on, whether on self-worth, relationships, parenting, communication, sexuality and work, only 10 per cent of the audience are men. It is not that men do not want to be there, but men are not providing the support for each other to open up to these essential aspects of living. Indeed, instead of the provision of mutual support, men tend to display cynicism, sarcasm, hostility and dismissiveness to opportunities to explore their inner and outer emotional and social worlds. It will certainly help if women encourage men's emancipation, but unless men shoulder each other it will be very difficult for them to discover the full expansiveness of being human. Women have learned the lesson of being a support to each other and know that the embracing and developing of the full range of human characteristics is vital to their gender; men still have this lesson to learn.

For the 10 per cent of men who dare to explore the taboo areas, interestingly, they are much more inclined to 'bite the bullet' on the issues raised. Part of the reason for this is that their predominantly masculine characteristics enable them to take on the difficult challenges, which largely revolve around their feminine side. The reverse is true for women; their masculine side has long been in chains and their feminine characteristics of inward movement, tenderness, nurturance, passivity and caring for others make it more difficult for them to progress in finding the needed balance between feminine and masculine human characteristics.

It is in the interests of both genders to no longer support the polarisation of men and women and to support each other in exploring the expansiveness of being fully human.

LIVING IN THE LIGHT

Light has long been a metaphor for such things as love, healthy living and spirituality. In the past hundred years, psychology, sociology and progressive medicine have discovered that the three essential ingredients for emotional, social and physical well-being are: love of self, love of others and love of life. Frequently the last one of the trilogy is not as promoted as the first two. Nonetheless, the frequently quoted maxim, 'seize the day', demonstrates that there is some realisation of the need to embrace life.

Recently, after a talk to a large group of second-level students, a quite unhappy-looking fourteen-year-old girl approached and asked me: 'What is the meaning of life?' Before I could answer, she said despairingly: 'Without meaning there is no reason to go on living.' I suspect she had a poor sense of herself and certainly did not feel loved for herself by the significant adults in her life. However, a public setting was not the place to explore these dark areas of her life. I thanked her for her question and went on to say that I felt there were two aspects to her query: 'What is living all about?' and 'Is there a deeper purpose to existence?' As regards the former I told her that I felt life was for living and that I hoped she would seize its every precious moment. As for the latter issue, I relayed that this was an age-old spiritual quest of human beings and one that could only be answered in her own heart and spirit. I did add that the more deeply and fully she lived life, the more likely the greater purpose of life would emerge for her. Finally, with a supportive and affectionate look into her eyes, I expressed my belief that giving and receiving love was the bedrock to loving life and discovering spirituality.

A lot more enthusiasm, excitement, fun and adventure seem to emerge in summertime. After a year's work for adults and the end of the school year and examinations for students, people are ready to seek out more of the joys of living. However, the pity is that work and learning have ceased to be fascinating challenges and the 'summer break' becomes the oasis in the desert of work and school lives. Kahlil Gibran's insight that 'work [and learning] is love made visible' is much needed to enlighten many home, work and school environments!

Nonetheless, there is no doubt that summer light, long days, warmth, blossoming nature, and silver and purple dazzling seas and rivers touch into the light of our being and provide the opportunities to enjoy the endless days of summer. I believe that it is the metaphorical meaning of light that connects with the spirit of people. It has to be seen too that the brightness of summer does not penetrate those individuals whose hearts and spirits have been darkened by emotional, social, spiritual, educational and political neglect.

There is a theory in psychiatry that the absence of sunlight causes a depressive condition known as Seasonal Affective Disorder (SAD). Special lamps that give artificial sunlight have been invented to help individuals who are affected by this problem. With respect to my psychiatric colleagues, I find the whole concept both naïve and in no way reflective of the depth, complexity and resourcefulness of human behaviour. There are far more serious reasons why people may become depressed in wintertime.

Like light, darkness has long been associated with the absence of light, the loss of love, meaning and spirituality.

'The dark night of the soul' is truly representative of this powerful metaphor. The dark of winter does not create depression, but touches into a darkness of life and spirit that is already within and without. When people experience enduring emotional rejection, it is tantamount to blowing out the light of a candle and plunging them into the blackness of a loveless life. Furthermore, in the shorter days and longer nights of winter, the darkness symbol predominates and there is also a lot more time to contemplate one's state. I believe that those who suffer the depression of SAD are unable to find their inner light and rely on the artificial lights of the outside world. It would be far more helpful for people living in shadow to have the enduring light of support, love, understanding, compassion, patience and nurturance brought to them by those of us who purport to care for their emotional, social and spiritual well-being. The more we connect with the light of our own being and living, the more we are in a position to help others to dispel the darkness of anonymity, alienation from others and fear of living.

PART FIVE
WORK

- ☐ Does our work control us or do we control it?
- ☐ The prestige professions
- ☐ Relationships and work
- ☐ Stress treadmill
- ☐ The fall of the vocation professions
- ☐ Workplace bullying
- ☐ Common sense at work

DOES OUR WORK CONTROL US OR DO WE CONTROL IT?

Everybody works. Some people go out to jobs; others take care of homes, children, the sick and the elderly; still others do the laundry, clean the house, prepare meals, take care of pets. Each person works at something. Whether we work at home or outside the home, work is an important part of our lives. It does not serve anyone when we are indifferent to the part that work plays in our lives. Work needs to be worthy of your person, dignity, energy and giftedness. When this ethos is present, you feel challenged, energised, visible, inspired and satisfied. There exists a healthy flow between your personal, interpersonal, family, recreational, spiritual and occupational lives and work contributes to your overall feeling of well-being.

The more common phenomenon is where work either takes over our lives or alienates us. When either of these situations is operating, important questions need to be asked and difficult decisions may need to be made.

If you feel work dominates your life, questions that need answering include:

- Does work make you feel sick?
- Does work control your life?
- Does your personal, family and social life suffer?
- Do you feel your identity is tied up with work?
- Do you fear failure?
- Are you addicted to success?
- Do you live in fear of criticism?

Positive answers to any of these questions indicate a need for changes in how you see yourself, how you view work and how the work organisation sees you. These are challenges that touch the heart of your personal, family and spiritual security.

When workers are addicted to, fear or hate work, it means that their earlier experiences of work led to a confusion between their individual worth and their work efforts. Children (and adults) deserve to be loved, valued and accepted for their unique person, individuality, differences and giftedness. However, what is more common is that children's behaviours become the determinants of parents, teachers and others demonstrating love to children or withdrawing it, sometimes harshly, when certain behaviours are not present or not executed to a desirable performance level. All infants love to learn and work, but the experience of being criticised, ridiculed and rejected because of poor behavioural performance gradually dries up their excitement around challenges. They learn cleverly and quickly to find ways of removing or reducing threats around learning and work. The most common means of reducing possibilities of hurt are perfectionism, avoidance, rebelliousness and sickness.

The solution lies in separating self from the experience of work; in so doing you restore self to its unique and sacred place and keep work in its place as one of the many challenging life experiences open to you. This may be a difficult aspiration to achieve on your own. It can help enormously if you join a support group for this process and even more so when workplaces facilitate and encourage such emancipation. The rewards are great for both the individual and the organisation — independence, high energy, ambition, creativity, increased productivity and job fulfilment.

Regrettably, many workers experience not only anonymity but alienation in their places of work. The culture and management style in such organisations can be hostile, overpowering, purely profit-focused and lacking in any regard for the personal, interpersonal and family needs of employees. Ironically, these organisations fail to tap into the individuality, creativity and vast potential of workers and, as a result, staff morale, motivation to work and productivity suffer greatly from such neglect.

If you feel that work is demeaning and the workplace is an alien place to be, you need to seriously examine this wearisome situation:

- Do you feel anonymous in the workplace?
- Is the work you do worthy and respectful of you?
- Is the management style aggressive?
- Is the work culture person or family friendly?
- Do you shrink from protesting about unfair practices?
- Do you feel hostile towards work?
- Does work threaten your sense of self?
- Do you feel scared in the workplace?

Workers deserve recognition, respect and an empowering style of management. They deserve an ethos that values person and family, allows expression of grievances, is emotionally and socially safe and friendly, and provides opportunities for the development of their unique skills and creativity. Where there is an absence of such care, workers are well advised to take stock of their situation and make decisions that are worthy of their dignity.

It is also the case that work organisations encounter major difficulties with workers who are frequently absent, do the least work for the most money, are hostile, difficult, resentful and undermining of more motivated workers, hate work, fear responsibility and frequently call in sick. In an era of high employment and legal restrictions, many employers are left floundering, not knowing what to do with workers who are falling short of reasonable expectations or who have become a major liability.

Certainly, work organisations benefit from workers who are mature and balanced in their approach to work, but they also gain, in the short term, from those workers who work hard to get everything right with no mind to time or to their personal or interpersonal lives. However, there is a downside to workers who are perfectionistic: they burn out, create difficult staff relationships and make poor leaders.

Like the over-worked or alienated worker, work organisations that are at the receiving end of workers who are either over-responsible or under-responsible need to take strong action to bring about a work environment that generates a fair day's work for a fair day's pay, creates high job satisfaction, provides opportunities for development of giftedness and instils a love of and excitement around work.

THE PRESTIGE PROFESSIONS

I have only recently returned from a business trip to South Africa, a country rich in beauty and potential but presently besieged by a 50 per cent unemployment rate. There is no doubt that the country is in a transition phase and, hopefully, the prophets of doom and gloom will be proved wrong. One of the consequences of unemployment there, similar to what it was in Ireland not so long ago, is brain drain. Many graduates in South Africa are now compelled to go abroad to pursue their careers. However, one of the things that alarmed me about the educational and social systems there is the presence of prejudice similar to that which still exists in Ireland towards the so-called 'prestige' professions – medicine, law, accountancy and, more recently, information technology. The sad consequences to this bias is that the individuals who conform to and succeed in these areas of accomplishment, and also those who go into the less-favoured occupations, will both suffer doubts about themselves and a lifetime of occupational and personal insecurity.

Those who 'succeed' and have been told how 'brilliant' they are become addicted to success and perfectionism, and they narrow their lives down to the area of their achievements. They tend to neglect their emotional, social, physical, sexual, creative, recreational and spiritual development. They often experience burnout at an early age. In South Africa, many young people are burning out in their early thirties; this phenomenon is also happening here in Ireland.

The main signs of burnout are:

- ☐ Absenteeism
- ☐ Physical exhaustion
- ☐ Appetite problems (undereating or overeating)
- ☐ Insomnia
- ☐ Psychosomatic complaints (headaches, back pain, chest pain, stomach or bowel problems, etc.)
- ☐ Irritability
- ☐ Reliance on drugs such as alcohol, tranquillisers, anti-depressants, nicotine
- ☐ Pessimism and fatalism
- ☐ Poor relationships with colleagues
- ☐ Feeling overwhelmingly threatened

Burnout results from the combination of the enmeshment of self with work and work pressures. The help that is needed is the separation of the person's sense of self from work and the development of a balanced approach to work. A supportive and family friendly workplace would greatly benefit this process.

What is often not recognised is that the child or adult who is told he is brilliant (because of academic or professional achievements) is more physically and emotionally at risk than the child or adult who is told he is a fool. At least the latter will not have many expectations made of him, but the former will put untold pressure on himself to maintain his 'success' status; to do otherwise would mean risking rejection. Nonetheless, those children and adults who have not attained the favoured professions will suffer feelings of inferiority for the rest of their lives unless they resolve these dependency issues.

Learning and work are precious aspects of our lives, but unless we as a society begin to value and celebrate equally all human endeavour, then we will continue to produce people who have either superiority or inferiority complexes.

Each person has an innate drive to manifest his or her uniqueness, difference, individuality and creativity. In the family and classroom every child will do all in their subconscious power to be different. It is a well-established fact that children within a family tend to go in opposite directions in terms of personality development. This is not a genetic process but an intelligent and creative process on the part of each child to express his or her own individuality. Children (and adults) are not passive recipients of what happens to them, but are clever active recipients and, in spite of demands for conformity, fight hard to express their individuality. If only parents and teachers would chart how each child reveals his unique identity in the behaviours and interests he shows and value and support and encourage that individualisation, they would gift children with the emotional, social and educational opportunities to live their own lives and manifest their own vast potential and unique giftedness. Work organisations would also do well to mark, support and reward individuality in the workplace.

In charting a child's or, indeed, an adult's ways of expressing their individuality, what often emerges are the career possibilities that the person would do well to pursue. Doing what you have a passion for is a way of matching your talents with a chosen profession. Doing what others expect of you is almost certain to result in an unhappy career choice. Sometimes it is useful to check back on what activities inspired you as a child and then look for a career that picks up on those activities.

When you have lost touch with your own voice, sometimes talking to a good career guidance counsellor may help you to reconnect with what inspired you in your early years.

RELATIONSHIPS AND WORK

From infancy, work affects our lives. Traditionally, father was missing from home from 8 a.m. to 6 p.m. and, in recent years, many mothers have adopted a similar pattern. Where work dominates a parent's life, leading to late homecomings and weekend work, it can have serious effects on family relationships. There is no intention here to suggest that parents should not work outside the home. It is not the quantity but the quality of the time parents spend with children that matters for their children's overall development. It is when parents make work more important than relationships that personal, couple and family problems arise. Furthermore, because children tend to imitate their parents, they too will develop a similar unhealthy focus on work or they may rebel and become apathetic around work.

Parents who run a family business can often have the illusion that because they are around the place they are there for their children, and they can be shocked when confronted with the reality that mere physical presence is not nearly enough for children (or adults) to feel loved, wanted and secure. Equally, parents who are absent from the home due to overworking can be dismayed when either partner or offspring complain of feeling invisible and unloved. These people believe that 'being the breadwinner' is a means of showing love. Emotional security is a product of the presence of affection, warmth, friendship, affirmation, encouragement, play and social outings. There have to be frequent, sincere and genuine interactions for the formation of relationships and high self-esteem.

Apart from partners or children feeling rejected when work appears to count more than they do, when parents over-focus on work it can lead to a situation where the children in turn learn to associate their own sense of self with work. Children will do anything to gain the love of their parents, and becoming the 'hard worker' can be a means of getting 'well-earned' attention. The problem is that these children will believe they must always 'be busy' in order to offset any possibility of criticism from their workaholic parents. I have worked with women who will never let their partners 'catch' them sitting having a cup of coffee or leafing through a magazine. They learned this protection at a young age and are now projecting the work expectations of their parents onto their partners. Most people choose a partner who resembles the parent who most influenced them, and if that parent modelled a strong work ethic then this is likely to be reinforced by their partner. I have also worked with men who have had huge difficulties in letting go of their role as 'breadwinner' because they dreaded subconsciously that rejection would follow such an action.

It needs to be seen also that parents who dislike or hate work affect their children's attitudes to work and that the couple relationship can suffer too. It would be difficult for a child to show ambition and eagerness to work in the face of a parent who complains constantly about work, comes home tired and irritable, and does not actively encourage them to love work. Neither would such a parent show strong interest in the child's educational development.

Because opposites attract, very often a person who tends to avoid, dislike or do minimal work marries a person who is perfectionistic, highly ambitious or addicted to work. The latter partner can be very critical of the 'malingerer', and vice versa. Disappointment, criticism and conflict can quietly eat into the heart of their relationship. It is very confusing and threatening for children when one parent discounts work and the other worships it. Unhealthy coalitions within the family can result from the tension created, with some of the children identifying with and becoming like the parent who finds work a threat to self-worth and the other children allying themselves with the parent who is addicted to work and following in that parent's perfectionistic footsteps.

It is sad when the worth of a person – child or adult – is seen to lie in their behaviour and not in their unique and wonderful being. Depending on the intensity of the work ethic in the home, children can develop major anxiety around work at home and in school. Parents often defend themselves by claiming that they never said verbally to their children they should work so hard, but actions always speak louder than words. It is the parents' own over-involvement with work that children imitate. To be fair to parents, workplaces typically have not been couple or family friendly. Minimal progress has been made in these areas. Society is constantly shouting about the sanctity and value of the family, but it rarely puts its words into action.

Individual adults can certainly address their own attitudes to work and ensure that they see their own person as infinitely more important than their work life and that couple and family relationships vastly outweigh the importance of any product. Employers would do well to create a supportive and family friendly work environment. This process would not mean in any way diluting the responsibilities of employees. It could mean that workers would feel more disposed towards executing their responsibilities. It certainly would bring about an emotionally and physically healthier workforce.

STRESS TREADMILL

As you read this chapter, are you totally absorbed in what you are reading or have you drifted to replaying in your mind unresolved work, family, relationship or personal issues? When people have difficulty living in the present and tend to live in the future or past, such behaviour would indicate a high level of stress.

Whilst stress has become a ubiquitous hazard in our hectic modern Ireland, leading to unhappiness, work absenteeism or work addiction, and, indeed, serious illness, it is not a new phenomenon. Stress is a relatively new word for human problems. The word 'stress' comes from the area of technology, and it means pressure or strain. It is a more benign word for human problems than old descriptions, such as 'she's suffering from the nerves' or 'he's neurotic'. Nevertheless, I believe my parents and other adults of their time were just as stressed as parents and other adults of today. Certainly, the external sources of stress have changed, but the internal ones of low self-esteem, fear, dependence, loneliness, depression and guilt are the same.

Work is definitely a major external source of stress. It is ironic that some fifteen years ago in the doom and gloom days of high unemployment, a three-day week and increased leisure time was predicted. In fact, the opposite has happened. So much for the prophets of doom! Instant electronic communication has elevated expectations, leading to increased educational, social and career pressures on the individual. In terms of work, many employees are packing the equivalent of a six-day week into their work, leaving less time available for family, marriage, intimacy, leisure, spirituality and themselves.

Some people will argue that a certain degree of stress is needed and, indeed, there is truth in that. However, it is important to make the distinction between healthy levels of stress and threatening levels of stress. Necessary stress is the apprehension experienced when taking on a new challenge or the tension needed to stand up or the digestive system responding to food intake, but when you worry about work so that your stomach is in a knot, or you stay on your feet without rest and you eat on the run, you are now in the realm of what I call emergency stress. The term 'emergency' is apt because when you go beyond the bounds of acceptable stress levels, you are in a distress cycle, and this means that you are physically, emotionally, socially and spiritually at risk. The higher the stress response, the greater the danger to your well-being. The alarm bells of the symptoms of stress are attempts to wake you up and get you back to a wellness cycle.

A wellness cycle is characterised by a strong sense of your worth, an independence of others, a love of work, a need for privacy, a balanced lifestyle and a respect and love for others.

A distress cycle is where a sense of your own sacredness has been lost, there is an enmeshment of self with what you do, a dependence on what others think of you, a fear of failure, an addiction to success and a dread of criticism. Clearly, these sources of stress are on a continuum, going from mild to extreme. The deeper and more intense your feelings of invisibility and dependence are, the greater the level of stress.

Stress symptoms are not always immediately obvious. While you may not be consciously aware that you are stressed, checking your body voice may well get you in touch with your stress levels. Physical symptoms include pains and aches, indigestion, tension, diarrhoea, constipation, asthma, migraines, skin conditions, fatigue, restlessness, frequent colds or flus and insomnia. When you look more deeply beyond the physical, you may notice increased irritability, impatience, rushing, racing, pessimistic attitude to work, troubled relationships, difficulties in concentrating, anxiety, loneliness, depression and fear.

There are many practical things you can do to reduce stress and to move towards a wellness cycle. Simple goals – such as eating healthily, regular rest breaks, doing things that you enjoy, being with people who are supportive and inspirational, confiding in someone who is unconditionally accepting of you – can certainly help to redress the balance. Regular physical exercise helps you to feel both physically and mentally alert. What is needed are moderate ways of exercising – walking, swimming, tennis, cycling – all of which are good for releasing tension, improving breathing and building up fitness.

When you are severely stressed a balanced life regime is anathema, but structuring your day and week is the first important step towards de-stressing. When you find, in spite of your best efforts, that you are unable to adhere to a balanced lifestyle, you would be advised to talk to an expert in the area of stress who will help you to detect the reasons why you are maintaining a neglectful lifestyle.

THE FALL OF THE VOCATION PROFESSIONS

The 'call' to religious life was once the wish of every parent for their son or daughter. The belief was that this call came from God, even though it was bandied about regularly that the vocation was more that of the mother than that of the young aspirant. Nevertheless, the vocation to the priesthood, sister-hood or brotherhood had the effect of making a privileged class out of those who answered the call, even though, within religious life itself, great neglect abounded of physical, emotional, sexual and social welfare. Individuality and difference were quashed and sameness was the norm. The drastic effects of this anonymity have been emerging over the last decade.

What is often forgotten is that there were other 'call' professions that have also suffered equal neglect and exploitation. Even though the 'call' was not seen as divinely located, the call to teaching and nursing had that vocational twist that implied that those called should deem themselves privileged. What underpinned the vocational professions was that one should not complain because one had the privilege of serving others – the sick, the mentally disturbed and children. To voice any needs was seen as selfish, and for long years passivity dominated the vocational professions. It is not then surprising in an era where the love of self is seen as the cornerstone for the love of others that nursing and teaching are no longer seen as attractive professions.

Today, there is an increasing shortage of both teachers and nurses, and thousands of nurses are being brought over from the Philippines. Excellent nurses and teachers have left their professions, because of an ethos that was manipulative and exploitative. Certainly, the 'handmaid' status of nursing, the poor salary, the major role demands, the powerlessness and limited career development finally resulted in an exodus from and a current poor level of application for the profession. Teachers have been similarly neglected in terms of increasing role demands, poor salary, second-highest pupil-teacher ratio in Europe, a punishing exam-directed education system and a great lack of back-up professional support. Staff relationships, ongoing professional development, students in distress, poorly trained managers, limited career opportunities and lowered status are examples of some of the areas that governments have consistently ignored. As a consequence, many wonderful teachers have left the system and are pursuing careers that are more appreciative of their drive, ambition and skills. Furthermore, the quality of graduates being attracted to the profession is not to the standard of previous years.

It is vital that the profile of the teaching profession is improved, not only in terms of qualifications, career opportunities, attractive salary, life-long professional development, but also in terms of status and power to shape an educational philosophy that is holistic in nature and not at the mercy of the tunnel vision of political and economic forces.

The three most important professions in society are parenting, teaching and nursing. It is regrettable that the first profession is still not recognised and that many parents are floundering in the raising of their children in a rapidly changing Ireland.

The school is the second home of children, and, in partnership with parents, needs to provide for the total development of children – physical, social, emotional, intellectual, educational, spiritual, sensual, recreational and occupational. Children deserve teachers who are highly motivated, well qualified, well-paid, well-mannered, who love children, have a manageable pupil-teacher ratio and are backed-up by educational psychologists, family therapists, counsellors, social workers, resource teachers, home-school liaison and effective leadership.

As much as the general public, the media or the government might like to ignore it, the present pay crisis is but the tip of the iceberg of an exploited and stressed profession. Research reliably shows that teaching is now the most stressful social occupation, above police officers, prison officers, medical doctors and dentists. The fallout from stress is not only the high level of stress-related illnesses, early retirement on stress and sickness grounds and the move to other professions, but the poor literacy and numeracy levels of a high percentage of school children. Some surveys have suggested that anything up to 50 per cent of teachers hate teaching. It is not possible for these teachers to inspire children with a love of learning.

WORKPLACE BULLYING

Typically, bullying has been seen as a phenomenon peculiar to schools, and slowly adults have begun to accept that children hurt other children in direct and indirect aggressive ways. Such hurting can also occur in homes. However, what many adults have not been prepared to look at is that children learn their bullying ways from adults, and that those children who bully are often victims of bullying from significant adults in their lives – parents, grandparents, childminders, teachers and older siblings. It is also the case that those children who are victimised are victimised by adults in the home.

Whilst there certainly has been a recognition that children can suffer physical and sexual neglect, society has not yet developed the maturity to accept that adults frequently emotionally hurt children. That adults emotionally hurt adults also demands recognition. Criticism, ridicule, dismissiveness, arrogance, hostile humour, gossiping, judging, comparing, superiority, verbal aggression, cynicism and sarcasm are examples of emotional hurting.

Within the last two years the newspaper spotlighting of allegations of bullying in the workplace has begun to raise awareness of the presence of psychological hurting. A difficulty arises with the defining of emotional bullying. Certainly, it is easier to define physical and sexual harassment. For example, a number of individuals I have helped to deal with bullying in the workplace were vague initially in their description of what was oppressing them, but, nonetheless, hated going to work. However, with help these individuals began to describe undue pressures to perform, lack of recognition of their responsible work efforts, anonymity, lack of appreciation of achievements and unrelenting pressure to do more and more. Bullying is not just about the presence but also about the absence of certain behaviours. Generally, work organisations do not have a back-up system to deal with neglect or a monitoring system that safeguards the emotional and social welfare of employees.

Other subtle, but insidious, forms of bullying are: not calling people by their preferred title, forgetting people's names, lack of promotional prospects, disrespect, being demeaning, putting down, stealing ideas, ignoring or ridiculing, double standards, inequality, unfair wages and unpaid overtime.

Clearly, there are more obvious ways of bullying in the workplace – not difficult to define – like humiliating, shouting, ordering, labelling, cynicism and sarcasm.

It is a sad fact that at least 40 per cent of managers still believe that the way to motivate workers is to bully them. What is even sadder is that those who bully do not consider that they are at fault in any way. The reason for that is that bullying is a defence behaviour, masking major insecurity, fear of failure or addiction to success. Subconsciously, those who bully are often driven to succeed and in the same way that they internally bully themselves into high work performance, they externally bully workers to attain high performance.

Organisations who do not deal with bullying eventually pile up problems for themselves. Not only is morale, creativity, productivity and initiative affected, but the effects of bullying – stress, anxiety, depression, sickness – lead to absenteeism and, sometimes, legal actions over claimed incidences of bullying.

A phenomenon that often occurs is that some employees who do become stressed, depressed, sick and absent do not associate their symptoms with the fact that they are being bullied. Sometimes, it takes somebody else to point out the incidences of bullying they have endured, and even then they may not assimilate the revelation. It is deeply humiliating for any adult to admit to being harassed and controlled by another adult and denial is a clever subconscious means of not having to face that reality. Sometimes there is an even deeper issue whereby that person was, as a child, bullied by a parent and the recognition of bullying in the workplace would lift the lid on the earlier experiences of rejection.

The following are warning signs of workplace bullying:

- Hate going to work
- High anxiety during working
- Depressive feelings
- Sudden bouts of crying
- Insomnia
- Loss of appetite
- Reliance on alcohol or tranquillisers
- Social withdrawal
- Psychosomatic symptoms (back pain, headaches, stomach problems)
- Talking obsessively about work

Since both those who bully and are bullied can be in a place of denial, it is incumbent on the work organisation to have definite structures in place to detect and deal with bullying. There are no organisations where bullying does not go on. Certainly, the frequency, intensity and endurance are important measures of the extent of the problem. Each organisation needs to ensure that their employees are treated as individuals, respected at all times and that work is worthy of each worker's dignity.

COMMON SENSE AT WORK

There are more books on management theory than there are pubs in Ireland. Common sense suggests that there are only so many ways of running an organisation. And common sense further dictates that if a new book on management theory is being published nearly every fifteen seconds, they can't be saying much that is different.

Many of the books employ some appalling jargon, such as 'staff retention' or 'task forces'! Furthermore, there was a time when we had personnel departments. Now they are called 'human resources' departments or, even more insultingly, 'HR'. My reaction to the term 'resources' is that it is something you dig out of the earth. The term 'human resources' reduces workers who are unique, sacred, different and who possess complex needs and emotions to mere 'resources'. Workers appear no more valuable than venture capital or raw materials. No wonder there is such a booming demand in clinical psychology, psychotherapy, psychiatry, counselling and homeopathy.

Job stress appears to be a growing phenomenon. A recent study found that 49 per cent of workers say their stress levels have got worse over the past twelve months. The Celtic tiger is creating a mental state called an 'amygdala hijack'. This is where the emotional part of the brain takes over, and the body releases adrenaline. The physical effect of this is to increase heart rate and blood pressure; in addition, blood is directed to the muscles and away from the digestive tract, causing irritable bowel syndrome, and from the immune system, hence the risk of cancer. It is well documented that prolonged stress can lead to psychological disorders such as depression, anxiety and insomnia as well as physical conditions such as migraine, indigestion, irritable bowel, high blood pressure, heart disease and even cancer.

Stress now accounts for over 70 per cent of visits to the GP and is one of the most common reasons for taking days off work, causing employers major loss of productivity.

There are many common sense responses that work organisations can make to offset job stress. The most important is to treat workers as human beings. There are so many employees who complain of alienation, anonymity and being treated like a cog in a machine. Both the presence and absence of each individual worker must matter, and work organisations need to find ways of recognising and respecting the individuality, worthiness, difference and potential of each worker. Such valuing and equality does not mean not confronting poor performance or not encouraging greater productivity, but it does mean that the person of the worker is not sacrificed on the altar of greater efficiency. The latter is the dilemma that faces work organisations – are products more important than workers or is it vice versa? When the 'human resources' department attempts to introduce a more person-centred approach, but workers intuitively pick up that the hidden or not so hidden agenda is greater efficiency, then sooner or later the staff rebel in one way or another. And rightly so! Respect for another human being must not be something that is earned but a response that is unconditional. Ironically, even though many employers are fearful of taking the risk, genuine acceptance of the unique presence of each worker inevitably leads to greater motivation, productivity and creativity. Sadly, there is still a strong belief among managers that the way to get the best out of workers is by bullying, criticism, verbal harassment, cynicism and sarcasm.

A second common sense response to stress in the workplace is for employers to give staff more room to enjoy their work. Instead of viewing sociability at work as a threat to efficiency and productivity, they should see it as a crucial ingredient. A good chat is the cement that holds organisations together.

Another practical innovation is to discover the emotional and social needs of workers. Employees come into the workplace with a wide range of needs and if these are ignored, dismissed or neglected, their motivation to work and cooperate with job demands will be adversely affected. The caring work organisation reaches out with heart and mind to its members and does it in a way that does not jeopardise the work goals of the organisation. On the contrary, the mature organisation knows that everybody gains when workers feel cherished.

PART SIX
WELL-BEING

- The meaning of illness
- The gift of being present
- Healthy humour
- Bodies talk
- Hard to swallow
- Understanding depression
- Tired and over-emotional
- The body is sacred
- There is more to back problems than pain!
- The nightmare of insomnia
- Which counsellor?

THE MEANING OF ILLNESS

The more I encounter and attempt to understand illness, the more I see the complexity of it. There is rarely one cause for illness and each case needs to be taken on its merits. What is certain is that no two illnesses, whether in two people or in one person at different times, are the same. Any evaluation needs to be holistic in nature, and the person who can tell you most about an illness is the person who is ill. However, in the current medical climate few patients are asked their opinion and the experience of having to lie back, be silent, take your diagnosis, prognosis and prescribed treatment is still far too common. This sometimes subconscious arrogance goes against considerable scientific evidence on the psycho-social and biospiritual nature of most diseases. However, when you are frightened and dependent, it is very difficult to voice your rights to ownership of your own mind and body.

From my own clinical experience I have formulated a number of basic understandings of illness:

☐ Sickness is but one of the many messages representing a time for emotional or social or physical or spiritual change, or some combination of these. Conscious awareness and action on these challenges can enhance the physical healing process.

☐ Emotional distress usually precedes physical distress. However, some people appear to need the presence of physical disease as a passport to revealing their inner and outer disharmony. This is not surprising as there is far more acceptance and sympathy available for physical disease than mental disease. Despite being told of the effects of stress on the body, many people do not think they will be the ones to become physically ill. The reason for such blindness is that making emotional and social changes may be highly threatening, even more so than illness. Physical illness is often a symbol, a metaphor, for a deeper emotional problem. For example, anorexia nervosa may symbolise the unexpressed need to be loved and nurtured and the emotional starvation that is present. Asthma may represent the constrictions on the expression of thoughts and feelings and the belief that, even if expressed, they will not be accepted.

□ The particular physical symptoms may be directly relevant to what is emotionally and/or socially amiss and may be an attempt to direct the person's attention to that area. For instance, the common complaint of back pain may be a message about 'taking too much on your back' or 'your back is against the wall' or 'you're backing out of certain responsibilities' or 'needing to deal with issues back there'.

□ The interpretation (best done in collaboration with the person who has the symptom) can be used to treat the body alone, or, when its deeper meaning is seen, to treat the whole person.

□ Secondary gain from illness blocks both physical and other healing and masks deep issues that the person is frightened of bringing to the surface. Secondary gain is where illness provides individuals with a way out of taking on responsibilities that are highly threatening to their sense of self. For example, an over-riding fear of failure can literally 'cripple' a person.

It is not my intention here to dismiss medical interventions. What I am advocating is a wide-angled view of disease, the participation of the client in the diagnosis and treatment, and the treatment not just of the physical disease, but of the whole person. Neither is there any suggestion that all illnesses are psycho-socio-spiritual-somatic, but each person who is ill deserves an intervention that is holistically focused. Disease by its very essence must effect change in the person, and this point is often misunderstood and even avoided by the person who is ill and by the medical practitioner.

The pity is that so many people get to the stage of serious illness before detection of long-term unresolved psycho-social problems. A holistic philosophy of prevention would go a long way to reducing the rate of illness. To date, most preventative programmes tend to focus on the physical issues of diet, exercise and lifestyle. What is required is a wider and deeper approach that makes it possible to talk out inner and outer conflicts. Men require permission to voice their inner feelings, and women need encouragement and support to ask for caring for themselves.

THE GIFT OF BEING PRESENT

Popular psychology and Buddhism lay strong emphasis on living in the present, being in the here and now, and leaving the past in the past and the future in the future. No matter what you are doing, the exhortation is to keep bringing your mind to the here and now and not give any attention to the thoughts, images and feelings that are to do with past experiences or future events. The implication is that being in the past or future are futile exercises and that happiness, peace and progress can only be achieved by living in the present.

Whilst I readily accept the good intentions of encouraging individuals to live in the now, my own experience is that it is much more realistic and progressive to be present to whatever is happening to you at any one moment. I do believe that the human mind, which has multiple physical, conscious, preconscious, subconscious and unconscious ways of expressing itself, does not present any action, thought, image, dream, feeling or intuition without a purpose. To drag yourself away from, say, bitter feelings and thoughts about some past traumatic experiences and compel yourself to focus on what is in the present, I believe violates the rightness of what is happening. It would appear a lot more sensible to acknowledge the wisdom of your reactions to the past event and to stay totally present to your feelings and thoughts. In doing so, you are likely to discover that there are unresolved issues to do with these past events and that your mind has cleverly found a way to bring your attention to them. One possibility is that you may need to talk out what you felt back then with the person who somehow darkened or demeaned your presence.

What you might well need to establish is the assertion of your independence and the redeeming of the power that was taken from you at that crisis time. In following through on the challenge that your mind has presented to you, you make further progress along the road less travelled back to your sacred presence.

Similarly, when your mind tends to be preoccupied with some future event – for example, a meeting, an interview, success at work, loss of a relationship, death – it would appear wiser to listen attentively to the message being presented, rather than disconnecting yourself by switching your attention back to some present activity, like meditation, relaxation, television. Living in the future is your mind's way of waking you up to the reality of being out of touch with your real self and being dependent on either persons or work or approval or success as measures of your value. What a wonderful challenge is presented to you when you stay with your agonising about the future. To dismiss the anxiety is to miss the opportunity for emotional and social progress. Attempts to resolve the dependencies being shown up are steps in the right direction of personal and interpersonal development.

I am not saying that practising meditation as a means of holding your attention on the present is an undesirable exercise, but it is vital that when any other thoughts, feelings or images arise you are present to them in order to discover their purpose. It is certainly true that at times we need to take a break from introspection, and relaxing in a hot, sudsy, aromatic bath or finding peace through visualisation, meditation or relaxation exercises are treats we all deserve. However, my own experience is that happiness is about staying in touch with what is happening, and progress is made by responding to the challenges that are involved in occasionally visiting your past or your future.

HEALTHY HUMOUR

Humour and pleasure can be tremendous stress buffers. In a world where stress is the main reason why people visit their doctors and where the six leading causes of death – heart disease, cancer, cirrhosis of the liver, lung ailments, suicide and accidental injuries – are directly or indirectly caused by stress, we need all the help we can get to maintain our health.

Just as the experience of pressure can trigger a stress response, the experience or anticipation of pleasure can elicit a wellness response. Several studies have shown that optimism is associated with longer life and less illness. We now know that merely watching a funny video or film alters our physiology beneficially. The old saying that 'laughter is the best medicine' makes sense in the light of this research.

An amazing story is told by Norman Cousins, an American journalist and writer, who in his early fifties began to experience paralysis and was diagnosed as having a debilitating brain disease for which there was no cure. He is a very personable man and is known for his philanthropy. Friends, colleagues, family and medical and nursing personnel were visibly upset by the pessimistic prognosis and Norman Cousins' experience was that they already had him dead and buried. He figured that if he did not get himself out of the hospital and away from all the well-meaning but pessimistic mourners he would certainly die. He came to believe that if he could create enough positive emotion and absent himself from hopelessness, he could break through the disease process. Even though at this point his tongue had become paralysed he got himself discharged from hospital, booked himself into a hotel room and got a friend to get him comedy videos, ones that he reckoned would elicit a belly laugh. He also dosed himself with Vitamin C. He would allow no visitors because they would come with their death masks. After five weeks he had his breakthrough and he experienced a full recovery against all medical expectations.

Certainly, humour played a part in his recovery, but I also believe his optimism and belief provided a major boost to his immune system, and this attitude gradually ate into the heart of his disease. Hope is essential to recovery.

There is now considerable evidence to back up Norman Cousins' use of humour. It has been shown that watching an hour-long comedy has positive effects on the levels of those hormones that are released during the classical stress response.

Research also shows that people who employ humour experience less fatigue, tension, anger, depression and confusion in response to stress. In other words, you are less affected by stress when you are able to recognise and use humour in your daily life.

There are a number of common sense reasons why humour has such positive effects on well-being:

- it gives you a break from ongoing stress and provides time for creatively altering your automatic stress response;
- it restores or replenishes depleted emotional resources;
- it acts to sustain you so you are better able to cope.

It is now well documented that stress is detrimental to the immune system, so it is good to know that the wellness effects of humour have been shown to enhance immune function. For example, among individuals reporting high daily stress and pressure, those who use humour to cope have higher levels of an infection-fighting substance known as immunoglobulin, compared to those who are humourless.

When humour is used as a coping skill it becomes much more than the funny story, a particular joke, a funny film, a skit; it becomes an expression of joy, hope, optimism, compassion, equanimity and playfulness in the face of a potential threat.

Humour is not a gift you either have or have not: it is a skill. Like any skill it improves with practice. Regrettably, our educational system does not view humour as an achievement, and I have never seen or heard of a child getting an A for humour. Nevertheless, some children are ingenious when it comes to humour, and in the long run these individuals may fare far better in life and health than those who are over-serious and academically driven.

BODIES TALK

Human beings are complex and each of us learns over the years to apply one layer of behaviour on top of another until our make-up is similar to that of an onion. In view of this, we all need to strive to find the inner core of ourselves and others and not be taken in by the outer covering. Whether you realise it or not, you rely on body language more than you think – to work out whether the plumber is overcharging you or whether your boss is telling the truth about the budget or whether the person you are interested in is only being polite or genuinely reciprocates your interest.

One way of assessing the truthfulness of your own or another person's behaviour is checking whether or not verbal behaviour matches non-verbal behaviour. When there is congruence, that is, an easy flow between mind and body, you can be relatively certain that authenticity is present. However, be wary of those people who practise body language techniques to camouflage their true intent. For example, sales representatives are good at smiling, making eye contact, steepling hands to convey confidence and sincerity and keeping palms open to appear honest. They also use the techniques of placing hands on coat lapels to convey solidity and to nod while telling a client about why they cannot do without a particular product. People tend to nod back automatically, making them more likely to take the bait.

Despite these sophisticated strategies, a closer look at the less than genuine salesperson's body language may reveal such inconsistencies as speaking too smoothly or being over-controlled or holding your gaze for far longer than seems natural or pupil dilation and blinking more rapidly than normal. For example, when President Clinton spoke about his affair with Monica Lewinsky, he blinked 120 times per minute. Two days later, when he gave a speech about an American raid on a terrorist group overseas, his blink rate was back to a normal 35 per minute.

There are more serious aspects to the reading and under-standing of body language and that is the revelation of hidden insecurities. Examples of body language that may reveal insecurities are:

□ Crossing arms across the solar plexus (waist)
□ Arms held tightly across the chest
□ Sullen expression
□ Winding leg several times around the other leg
□ Hand over mouth when speaking
□ Furrowed brow
□ Clenching hands tightly together until knuckles appear white

Individuals with any of these tendencies feel that it is some-how not safe to reveal their personal, relationship or work difficulties, but an astute and empathic observer could provide the opportunity for them to express their difficulties. Sensitivity to how they may receive your observations is essential. It is easy to offend people by innocently commenting on their words and actions. They may then feel more vulnerable and even judged and may refuse to cooperate with further questions. A direct approach such as asking: 'Do you notice at all how your leg keeps jerking'? is likely to provoke embarrassment or aggression. A much more understanding and caring approach is to silently recognise that the person is subconsciously manifesting some level of insecurity and to make efforts to be respectful and affirming of the person's unique presence and to be encouraging and supportive of their contributions.

It is also wise to realise that only the individuals themselves know the real causes of their involuntary body movements and this is a knowledge they may not yet be ready to consciously express and resolve. People in distress need to first open the door and invite you in as a support to facing their life difficulties. A rule of thumb that is worth remembering is to never give advice or make comments unless requested. Even when requested, be sure to respond tentatively: 'Well, the way I would see it . . . but I'm sure you know best yourself.' However, if no request is made, it doesn't mean that you should not show concern or express dissatisfaction or satisfaction. On the contrary, you should address the issue, but be determined to speak about yourself and not the other person. For example, 'I find it very difficult and embarrassing when in company you constantly fidget'. Be sure you do it quietly, without judgment and be sure that you put the emphasis on some need you have of the person.

Self-observation of your own body language is an essential step to understanding yourself and seeing the many layers of protection against hurt and humiliation that you have cleverly developed. Hiding behind these protective layers is your true self. However, if change is highly threatening to you, you are unlikely to be open to getting in touch with your own body talk. In these circumstances, a further protection is to be more interested in the body talk of others.

HARD TO SWALLOW

The loss of inner balance typically manifests itself in the body as a symptom. The symptom is both a signal and a vehicle for information, for its appearance interrupts life's familiar flow and compels us to give the symptom our attention. The symptom alerts us to the fact that we have lost our inner psychological balance. The symptom tells us something is missing. The symptom is not the great enemy; rather it is a kind of teacher, helping us to take responsibility for our own development and any lack therein. The discovery of what is lacking is the real challenge. Illness knows only one goal: to make us become whole.

For example, it may be the case that you are having difficulty swallowing. A symptom that is on the increase is a swallowing disorder. 'A lump in the throat' is one of the most common types of swallowing disorders and has no physical cause. People complain of a lump in the throat that comes and goes. Weight loss, social phobia and nutritional deficiencies are common consequences of this symptom.

Swallowing is a form of integration, of ingestion: in other words, to swallow is to incorporate. Once we have swallowed it down, it is no easy matter to reverse the process. Big pieces, meanwhile, we find 'hard to swallow'. There are many occasions in life when we have to swallow things that we would rather not – unwelcome pieces of information, for example. There is plenty of bad news or sad events that make us 'swallow hard'. The language of the throat can often be revealed through speech – 'something is stuck in my throat' when there is fear of speaking out; 'there is a lump in my throat', which frequently relates to unspoken grief; or there may be a continual need to clear the throat as if about to speak.

Rubbing the throat during a conversation can represent something that is painful and difficult to express. At other times, a hand placed over the mouth may be an effort to stop or muffle words coming out that may not be accepted. People who are inclined to blush may find that their redness stops as it reaches the neck; this may signify a desire to speak, but also a fear of creating disharmony with those concerned. It can also be the case that those who do not want to accept new ideas or who find change difficult will wear tight clothing at their necks or surround this area with scarves and high collars. There are those who 'bite their tongue' both physically and metaphorically and need to learn to let go. Grinding of the teeth at night suggests inner frustrations that are being stored in the subconscious during the day, only emerging during sleep.

Individuals who experience any of the above throat symptoms would do well to ask themselves: What is it in my life that I am currently unable or unwilling to swallow?

About two years ago I was in Northern Ireland doing a series of seminars, and on the first night in the hotel restaurant I nearly choked on a piece of steak. Fortunately, a soldier in plain clothes recognised my distress and performed the Heimlich manoeuvre, which saved my life. Later I asked myself what the frightening swallowing problem had been attempting to communicate. The answer came as clear as day: 'You are trying to bite off more that you can chew!' I was certainly taking on too many work commitments, thereby upsetting my inner psychological balance. The symptom was a clear wake-up call.

It can be very helpful for people who exhibit swallowing problems to keep a journal or write down any thoughts before going to bed – such actions certainly help to relieve tensions and aid sleep and recuperation.

UNDERSTANDING DEPRESSION

I met a young woman recently who has been in and out of both private and public psychiatric hospitals since the age of sixteen. She is now twenty-one. She has made several suicide attempts and periodically becomes obsessed with ending her life. Psychiatrists have told her there is no obvious precipitant for her depression – such as sexual abuse, physical violence, parents' separation – and that therefore she has a biological depression. They have advised her to stay on anti-depressant medication for the rest of her life. Ironically, the medication appears to have done little for her over the years. Suicide ideation and despair continue. Isolation from parents, siblings and peers is persisting. She also feels unable to leave home to go to college or work. Furthermore, the hopeless biological diagnosis and prognosis has in turn left her feeling hopeless, and she declares: 'What's the point in living if I have this incurable depression? How can I hold down a job, a relationship, get married, have a family, take on a mortgage, with this interminable millstone around my neck?'

One of the positives that the psychiatrist pointed out to her parents is that 'she loves to listen to music'. What is sadly fascinating is that the major reason for her depression can be detected in the lyrics of the music she constantly plays. Because of her biological mind-set there is no expansive listening occurring in this young woman's experiences. The song she most likes to listen to has the line 'I wish I was special, but I'm a creep', which projects very clearly her strong sense of worthlessness and invisibility.

There is nothing darker than not having a sense of your own value, sacredness, uniqueness and vast potential to understand the world you live in. Both of this young woman's parents have grave self-worth difficulties and neither were in a position to inspire their daughter with an acceptance and celebration of herself. Whilst there was no single major neglectful experience – such as sexual abuse or violence – there was the day to day experience of invisibility due to lack of contact by one parent and unrealistic expectations by the other. It is not only adults who experience 'lives of quiet desperation'.

My own clinical experience of people who present with depression is that there are always psychosocial reasons for their condition and that a holistic exploration with them of their unique biographical histories inevitably reveals patterns of relationships that explain the depression.

Getting to the causes does not lift the depression, but the breaking of the silence and the witnessing by me of the blocking experiences to the real expression of self is an important stepping stone. It is vital that a strong connection is established between the psychologist and the young person, so that the young person knows and feels that there is one person who is there for him or her. The involvement of parents is crucial, and my own experience is that the majority of parents more than willingly cooperate in their offspring's discovery of self and his or her need to be loved and accepted by them. Indeed, very often the young person's crisis is the catalyst for the parents to own and take responsibility for their own darkened sense of self and the troubled relationships between themselves and their children.

There is no intention here to blame parents or other significant adults for the lives of those who are depressed. Parents, teachers, relatives and siblings always do their best within the confines of their own vulnerabilities. You can only bring children to the same level of development that you have reached yourself. Nevertheless, while parents are not responsible *for* their child's depression, they are responsible *to* the behaviour they have perpetrated that, sadly though unwittingly, has darkened the presence of their son or daughter.

It is not an easy task for parents or others to face the shadow inside themselves and own the fact that their personal darkness begets darkness in their children. The light of honesty, openness, expression of regret, declaration of unconditional love and the presence of understanding, support, patience, compassion and encouragement can go a long way to helping their unhappy offspring emerge from the shadows of depression.

TIRED AND OVER-EMOTIONAL

Emotions are neither 'good' nor 'bad'. They are a form of expression that are only relevant to the particular situation in which they are found. Love, joy, excitement, anger, sadness, resentment, jealousy are all part of human nature. They are part of who we are. What is vital is that we do not allow our emotions to rule our lives, whether they are expressed or suppressed or repressed. People may become over-identified with their feelings.

Some people are labelled as 'emotional'. This usually means that they are easily brought to tears, although other emotions may be just as evident, such as anger, depression, happiness, jealousy or resentment. When questioned about their state of well-being, they will reply: 'I'm depressed', 'I'm happy', 'I'm angry', 'I'm resentful', 'I'm anxious'. Such statements, if repeated many times by self or others (e.g. 'you're depressed', 'you're anxious') begin to create an identity rather than a state of being at that time. 'I'm a depressive', 'I'm an anxious person', 'I'm a happy person', I'm an angry person'. It would be more accurate to say: 'At this moment I am feeling depressed'.

Emotions and feelings are there to be registered, and then to be employed for the purpose of learning and understanding why they occur. Once the feeling has been registered it needs to be released. If I feel depressed, I register the depression and then ask myself: 'My depression represents an energy block that needs to be released, so what can I do to alter the situation?' The solution may be physical or it may require changing the way I view a particular experience.

Being aware of and registering our emotions is not always easy, but it is helpful to develop a sense of self-worth, and to look to family or friends for support. Such inner or outer support allows the mind to attain a state of peace from where the answer will come.

Physically there may not be an easy solution, for example, grieving is a natural process of 'letting go' and requires time, but there may come a time when grief turns into self-pity. Such a state is blocking both to those who have suffered and to those around them. In such a case it may be necessary to come to terms with the situation and to accept that this is 'the way things are'. Such acceptance frees the individual to move forward, albeit tentatively to begin with.

I have encountered many situations where over-expression of the emotions hides a fear of change and a clinging to past beliefs. Such individuals are stuck in a rut and this may manifest itself physically in conditions where there is immobility such as osteoarthritis or in some of the neurological diseases. In such cases the prospect of change is more threatening to well-being than even physical illness. The clever, though sad, protection is 'I'm too busy being emotional to think about changing'.

There are some people who appear happy being depressed. They seem to thrive on their misery and enjoy regurgitating past hurts, let downs and resentments. Early on in life they may have found that the one way to be certain of attention was to complain. Conversely, sometimes people who are permanently 'happy' may be avoiding looking too deeply inside for fear of finding their vulnerability.

Many caring individuals have made great efforts to attempt to bring a friend, colleague or client out of their 'emotional' state, whether it is apathy, anger, depression, anxiety, resentment or happiness that masks insecurity. Often, the more those who tend to rescue try, the more their target goes the opposite way. Sometimes those who help become victimised, trapped in the web created by the original 'victim', leading to immobilisation for both individuals. At other times those who rescue end up marching off in frustration and disgust, and this reveals the underlying motive of the abortive attempt, which is to change someone else rather than look at their own need to change.

We cannot change others or carry them along their path or ours. What we can do is offer love and support. It is also productive to encourage them in those areas of their lives that are lacking, rather than trying to discourage their emotional state, without which they would feel totally insecure.

THE BODY IS SACRED

The physical body is sacred and unique and it houses your unrepeatable and individual human spirit. It must therefore be treated with the respect that any sacred object deserves. Any physical violence or neglect or criticism of an individual's human form is a violation not only of their physical presence but also of their spiritual sacredness.

It is estimated that the human heart has the capability to survive four hundred years; man or woman can destroy it in forty years. It is saddening that our physical bodies are employed to carry not only all the good things in life but also all our bitterness, jealousy, resentment, fears, hurts and hate. These forms of pollution ruin our temple far sooner than any external pollution.

The physical body possesses an amazing range of talents, such as agility, flexibility, intuition, strength, regeneration, transformation, creativity, extreme sensitivity and a very efficient communication system. The body relies on optimal physical, emotional, social and spiritual nourishment. Physical nourishment is healthy food, clean air, sound sleep, fitness, exercise, warmth, shelter, rest, comfort and ease. Emotional nurturance is the receiving and giving of love and the freedom to express all feelings. Social caring has got to do with recognition and respect for each person's uniqueness, individuality and difference, provision of opportunities for each person to express and develop their potential and giftedness, the presence of equality, justice and fair distribution of wealth.

Ultimately, each one of us is responsible for our own physical well-being; however, it helps enormously when the social systems we inhabit – home, school, community, church, workplace, sports clubs – create environments that dignify each person's presence. However, the reality is far from the ideal. Unfair practices, exploitation, anonymity, unfair expectations, manipulation, control and bullying are common experiences in social systems. Obviously, the frequency, intensity and duration of these demeaning responses is a crucial consideration. The bottom line is that your dignity should not be lessened in any of the social systems of which you are a member; when your dignity is compromised then difficult decisions need to be made.

When it comes to personal responsibility, we all need to check our attitudes to our bodies. It is still a sad fact that many women from many different cultures and countries feel badly about their bodies. Many women and, indeed, men feel that their bodies lack intrinsic beauty and value and a lot of effort can go into the correction of such distorted images of self. The cosmetic and plastic surgery industries have exploited this vulnerability.

For a moment, imagine something you prize, something you see as beautiful, unique and essential to your life; imagine what you would feel and do if someone treated that sacred object with callousness or disrespect or violence. Probably immediate outrage – a 'no' that would explode from deep within, born of a fierce sense of belonging and passion.

To recover your love of your body, you have to learn about it, re-acquaint yourself with it and see the truth instead of a distorted image. You need to look at the mirror within, not the external mirror of other people's view of you. Contrary to what most people think, beauty is *not* in the eye of the beholder, but in the eye of the beheld.

Loving your body is reflected in the following actions:

- ☐ Not exercising/working beyond tiredness
- ☐ Healthy diet
- ☐ Responding proactively to pain
- ☐ Regular exercise
- ☐ Playing
- ☐ Enjoying closeness with another person
- ☐ Attending to your intuition (gut reaction)
- ☐ Crying when you want to
- ☐ Experiencing joy when you want to
- ☐ Reading about your body
- ☐ Breathing deeply
- ☐ Singing
- ☐ Looking in the mirror with pride
- ☐ Laughing
- ☐ Objecting to any attempt by another to demean your or another's body
- ☐ Asking for a massage
- ☐ Stretching your body
- ☐ Regularly exercising your body
- ☐ Resting
- ☐ Resting
- ☐ Resting

Finally, both men and women need to honour the symptoms of their sacred bodies as allies to awakening them to the deeper emotional, social and spiritual neglect that might be going on.

THERE IS MORE TO BACK PROBLEMS THAN PAIN!

Stress now accounts for most illnesses and loss of time at work. Pressure can arise from either internal or external sources. The most common stress complaint is back pain. Up to 60 per cent of people in the West experience 'sudden' back pain at some stage, and, for at least 50 per cent of these, it becomes a continual or recurrent condition. Not surprisingly, back pain accounts for more absenteeism from work than any other stress condition.

Back pain generally results when a joint connecting two vertebrae is strained, by lifting something heavy, for example. 'Slipped disc' operations have now become a rare phenomenon, thanks to the recognition of the psychosomatic nature of back pain and, indeed, the very infrequent occurrence of an actual slipped disc.

Typically, people look for physical explanations for back pain and do not look to possible deeper issues that may underlie it. Certainly, those whose work is physical or sedentary appear more susceptible. Also people who are tall, elderly or overweight appear to be at higher risk. I deliberately use the word 'appear' even though other experts would be more definite in their categorisation of at-risk groups. The question that tugs at my ankles is why is it that only a certain small percentage of an 'at-risk' group of people suffer? I believe a holistic assessment of any stress symptom is needed if a long-term resolution of back pain is to be achieved. I am not suggesting that some back problems cannot result from physical strain, such as prolonged bending, strenuous exercise, poor posture, pregnancy and infections. However, I am encouraging that a wide-angled assessment lens be employed, particularly with a recurrent condition.

From my own experience of excruciating bouts of lower back pain over several years, I know that the causes were my 'taking too much on my back', 'getting my back up' about work and 'backing away' from conflict. It was the resolution of these psychological issues that led, eventually, to rare experiences of back pain. Every now and again the back pain recurs, but I notice the signs much earlier now and I quickly take corrective physical action. Following the physical intervention I then check if I have fallen back into my old ways.

Back pain is not an enemy, but an ally. Whether the causes are purely physical, psychological, social or occupational, the purpose of the pain is to wake you up to some neglect of self that you are perpetrating.

When you consider the possible metaphorical rather than literal significance of back pain, it is easier to detect possible causes other than purely physical ones. Metaphor is that marvellous language that we possess that can compress complex issues into a simple image. The word 'back' can symbolise so much of what we do in terms of how we neglect ourselves physically, psychologically and socially:

- □ 'you feel your back is against the wall'
- □ 'you back out of responsibilities'
- □ 'you put too much of your back into things'
- □ 'you take too much on your back'
- □ 'you get your back up about things'
- □ 'you engage in back biting'
- □ 'you are constantly uptight'
- □ 'you back off from confrontation'

- □ 'you feel rejected when you're not backed up'
- □ 'you tend to be stiff-necked about issues'
- □ 'you back out of conflict'

The point is that our emotional state manifests itself in our bodies in a meaningful way. For example, job and success addictions can cause individuals to neglect self, relationships and family, often leading to back pain, due to people being uptight about work and taking too much on their backs.

Certainly, with the onset of back pain it is important to find immediate physical relief. Conventional treatments involve rest and painkillers, with gentle exercise and manipulation. Treatment can also involve anti-inflammatory and muscle-relaxing drugs. Complementary therapies have become very popular, such as osteopathy, chiropractic, acupuncture, massage and the Alexander technique.

Both the medical and alternative therapies focus on eliminating or reducing the symptoms, and in the short term such treatments are beneficial. In the long term it is important to find the causes by seeing the metaphorical significance of the pain.

THE NIGHTMARE OF INSOMNIA

Sleep deprivation is akin to food deprivation and when either of these conditions is long-term they can seriously threaten your health.

We get our energy from two main sources – food and sleep. Sometimes people's fatigue problems may be due to missing meals, eating junk food, eating on the run, lack of fitness and a reliance on stimulants such as alcohol, caffeine or prescribed 'uppers'.

It is also the case that daytime exhaustion may stem from rushing and racing, pressure of work, stress, anxiety and depression. All of these latter experiences lead to difficulty in relaxation and inability to sleep, leading to a spiralling of feelings of exhaustion.

There is evidence that a considerable number of adults, at least one in three, for some weeks, even months, suffer from chronic insomnia. Research indicates that continual broken sleep or chronic sleep deprivation can lead to major anxiety, burnout, depression, intense irritability, and weakening of your immune response.

As in the case with all psychosomatic conditions, the causes of insomnia are unique to each person and generalisations need to be viewed with caution. Certainly, possible causes can be physical, psychological, social, occupational, physical, financial and existential, or some combination of these areas of functioning. Examples under each heading may help you to identify your specific reasons for showing sleep difficulties:

- Physical – pain, over-tiredness, hormonal changes, indigestion, post-traumatic stress;
- Psychological – preoccupation with inner doubts about self, worries about the future, dread of failure, addiction to success, depression, anxiety, living in the past, living in the future;
- Social – marital, relationship problems, family difficulties, separation, divorce, separation from children, baby who is not sleeping at night, hostile neighbours;
- Occupational – major pressures at work, hate work, dread work, feel sick at the thought of going to work, bullying at work, shift-work;
- Financial – worrying about not being able to make ends meet, major debts to be paid;
- Existential – fear of dying, despair, fear of living.

The crucial issue when you suffer from chronic insomnia is that, paradoxically, it is a wake-up call; the symptom is attempting to bring your attention to some actions that are needed for you to return to a wellness cycle. The body is always right and rather than seeing sleeplessness as a threat, embrace it as a friendly indication that some changes are needed in your life. Sometimes it may take some time to detect and resolve the causes of the insomnia, but in the meantime there are some practical things you can do to make it more likely you will get some sleep.

The first practical thing to realise is that you cannot make yourself sleep. Sleep is an autonomic activity, something you cannot make happen. Indeed, when you attempt to bring on sleep, you are only waking yourself up more. However, what is under your control is the capacity to rest and relax. The last thing to think about when you go to bed is sleep, but do focus on putting your body and mind at rest. Consider learning meditational methods, yoga, muscular relaxation or self-hypnosis from trained practitioners.

Other practical tips are:

- No television or computer in the bedroom
- Physically exercise sometime during the day, but not at night
- Dine before 7.00 p.m.
- Avoid stimulants after 9.00 p.m. – tea, coffee, alcohol, smoking
- Drink or take some soporific before bedtime – calcium supplement, hot milk, Horlicks, herbal tea (chamomile, passion-flower or lemon balm)
- Maintaining a regular routine time of retiring and rising aids the biological clock
- When thoughts keep going around in your mind, sit up and write them down and just note what actions you may need to take

If the above regimen does not help and if there are problems in your life that are going to take some time to resolve, then a visit to your family doctor for some sleeping tablets is advisable. However, be wary of using drugs as a substitute for resolving the causes of insomnia.

WHICH COUNSELLOR?

It wasn't so long ago that going to a clinical psychologist or counsellor was seen as a major source of threat. It is still the case that the last 'ologist' that a person requiring help is sent to is a psychologist. This is not surprising, given the difficulties our culture continues to have with personal vulnerability and the expression of emergency feelings (anger, depression, despair, anxiety, jealousy).

There is no doubt that men are more blocked in seeking affective help than women, but it has taken women a long time to wake up to their rights to be loved and seek help for their inner and outer conflicts. In many ways, women are still only at the tip of the iceberg in terms of exploring the depths of the emotional, social, sexual, occupational, religious and political oppression they have endured.

The primary source of depression is oppression, and this explains why women have tended to exhibit more depression than men. Do not get me wrong here, for men have also been oppressed, but not as extensively as women. Men's oppression has certainly been emotional and social, but they have had a lot more power than women in the social, occupational, religious, political and sexual fields.

It is a healthy development that both men and women (more women than men, it has to be said) are seeking psychosocial help and are relying less on medical interventions to cope with their difficulties in living. Historically, it was never a good development that people in emotional and social distress came under the umbrella of general medicine. Whilst I have no difficulty with short-term psychotropic medication, it needs to be seen that medication is not a therapy but only a symptom reducer. The underlying conflicts continue to lurk below the 'tranquillity surface' that medication creates, and will resurface as clients become tolerant to the toxic cocktail. Resolution of these conflicts can only be done by confronting those inner and outer demons. Such confrontation may need to be done with the support of a clinical psychologist or counsellor. However, many people seeking help are somewhat confused by the array of different kinds of therapies and helpers available.

For my own part I have stopped using the word 'therapist' because it suggests that it is the helper who has the power to change the client's life and not the client himself. Also I am uncomfortable that the word 'therapist' can be broken down to 'the-rapist'. In any case the idea of a 'therapist' is very much a misnomer. The truth is that only those seeking help can undertake the challenge of change and face the painful blocks to their progress in life. Nobody can do it for them. It is the failure to broadcast this that has led to much of the confusion and disillusionment for which dynamic psychiatry and psychotherapy have been responsible.

Experience has taught me that every client is different, with a unique biographical history; each client's symptoms are representative of his or her story and have no generalised meaning. My response needs to be a unique one and I hesitate at recommending any particular type of counselling to a client. Research has shown that effective helping is a function of the personal qualities and maturity of the helper, rather than the type of counselling he or she practises. The bottom line is that each client needs a different kind of helping.

There are certain characteristics of an effective professional helper:

- The ability to love the client unconditionally.
- The ability to actively listen with both mind and heart.
- The ability to communicate belief in the client's vast potential and giftedness.
- The provision of hope so that the client sees that the helper believes that change is possible.
- The openness to self-disclosure on one's own life journey.
- The communication of understanding so that the client feels secure in revealing his or her actions and innermost thoughts, feelings, images and dreams.
- The provision of safety and support and the calm management of the major suffering that may emerge.
- The ability to empathise and show compassion when hurt, rage, guilt or heart-rending sadness rise to the surface.
- The professional helper needs also to communicate that the presenting difficulties of an adult, adolescent or child are responses to the past and present social contexts of his or her life. Because of this, it is more accurate to say that all personal coping problems are psychosocial in nature and that is not just the inner life of the client that requires exploration. This may mean helping clients to separate out from social contexts – home, workplace, school, community, church – that have been instrumental in blocking their progress in life. It also means, whenever possible, inputting into these cultures that subconsciously darkened the presence of the person seeking help.